The Changing Face of Empire

SPECIAL OPS, DRONES, SPIES, PROXY FIGHTERS, SECRET BASES, AND CYBERWARFARE

BY NICK TURSE

Haymarket Books
Chicago, Illinois

Dispatch Books

© 2012 Nick Turse

Published by
Haymarket Books
P.O. Box 180165,
Chicago, IL 60618
773-583-7884
info@haymarketbooks.org
www.haymarketbooks.org

ISBN: 978-1-60846-310-7

Trade distribution:
In the U.S. through Consortium Book Sales
and Distribution, www.cbsd.com
In the UK, Turnaround Publisher Services, www.turnaround-uk.com
In Canada, Publishers Group Canada, www.pgcbooks.ca
In Australia, Palgrave Macmillan, www.palgravemacmillan.com.au
All other countries, Publishers Group Worldwide, www.pgw.com

Special discounts are available for bulk purchases by organizations
and institutions. Please contact Haymarket Books for more information
at 773-583-7884 or info@haymarketbooks.org.

This book was published with the generous support of the Wallace Global
Fund and the Lannan Foundation.

Printed in Canada by union labor on recycled paper containing 100 percent postconsumer waste in accordance with the Green Press Initiative,
www.greenpressinitiative.org.

Library of Congress CIP Data is available.

1 3 5 7 9 10 8 6 4 2

Table of Contents

1. The Changing Face of Empire   1

2. Uncovering the Military's Secret Military   11

3. America's Empire of Drone Bases   21

4. Arming Mideast Autocrats   33

5. The Pentagon's Training Missions   41

6. Prisons, Drones, and Black Ops in Afghanistan   49

7. Shadow Wars in Africa   57

8. Washington Puts Its Money on Proxy War   67

9. How the United States Creates Global Instability   79

10. What the U.S. Military Can't Do   91

A Note on the Text   97

The Changing Face of Empire

1.

The Changing Face of Empire

It looked like a scene out of a Hollywood movie. In the inky darkness, men in full combat gear, armed with automatic weapons and wearing night-vision goggles, grabbed hold of a thick, woven cable hanging from a MH-47 Chinook helicopter. Then, in a flash, each "fast-roped" down onto a ship below. Afterward, "Mike," a Navy SEAL who would not give his last name, bragged to an Army public affairs sergeant that, when they were on their game, the SEALs could put 15 men on a ship this way in 30 seconds or less.

Once on the aft deck, the special ops troops broke into squads and methodically searched the ship as it bobbed in Jinhae Harbor, South Korea. Below deck and on the bridge, the commandos located several men and pointed their weapons at them, but nobody fired a shot. It was, after all, a training exercise.

All of those ship-searchers were SEALs, but not all of them were American. Some were from Naval Special Warfare Group 1 out of Coronado, California; others hailed from South Korea's

Naval Special Brigade. The drill was part of Foal Eagle 2012, a multinational, joint-service exercise. It was also a model for — and one small part of — a much publicized U.S. military "pivot" from the Greater Middle East to Asia, a move that includes sending an initial contingent of 250 Marines to Darwin, Australia, basing littoral combat ships in Singapore, strengthening military ties with Vietnam and India, staging war games in the Philippines, and shifting the majority of the Navy's ships to the Pacific by the end of the decade.

That modest training exercise also reflected another kind of pivot. The face of American-style war-fighting is once again changing. Forget full-scale invasions and large-footprint occupations on the Eurasian mainland; instead, think: special operations forces working on their own but also training or fighting beside allied militaries (if not outright proxy armies) in hot spots around the world. And along with those special ops advisors, trainers, and commandos expect ever more funds and efforts to flow into the militarization of spying and intelligence, the use of ever more drone aircraft, the launching of cyber-attacks, and joint Pentagon operations with increasingly militarized "civilian" government agencies.

Much of this has been noted in the media, but how it all fits together into what could be called the new global face of empire has escaped attention. And yet this represents nothing short of a new Obama doctrine, a six-point program for twenty-first-century war, American-style, that the administration is now carefully developing and honing. Its global scope is already breathtaking, if little recognized, and like Donald Rumsfeld's military lite and David Petraeus's counterinsurgency operations, it is evidently going to have its day in the sun — and like them, it will undoubtedly disappoint in ways that will surprise its creators.

The Blur-ness

For many years, the U.S. military has been talking up and promoting the concept of "jointness." An Army helicopter landing Navy SEALs on a Korean ship catches some of this ethos at the tactical level. But the future, it seems, has something else in store. Think of it as "blur-ness," a kind of organizational version of warfighting in which a dominant Pentagon fuses its forces with other government agencies — especially the CIA, the State Department, and the Drug Enforcement Administration — in complex, overlapping missions around the globe.

In 2001, Secretary of Defense Donald Rumsfeld began his "revolution in military affairs," steering the Pentagon toward a military-lite model of high-tech, agile forces. The concept came to a grim end in Iraq's embattled cities. A decade later, the last vestiges of its many failures continue to play out in a stalemated war in Afghanistan against a rag-tag minority insurgency that can't be beaten. In the years since, two secretaries of defense and a new president have presided over another transformation — this one geared toward avoiding ruinous, large-scale land wars which the U.S. has consistently proven unable to win.

Under President Obama, the U.S. has expanded or launched numerous military campaigns — most of them utilizing a mix of the six elements of twenty-first-century American war. Take the American war in Pakistan — a poster-child for what might now be called the Obama formula, if not doctrine. Beginning as a highly-circumscribed drone assassination campaign backed by limited cross-border commando raids under the Bush administration, U.S. operations in Pakistan have expanded into something close to a full-scale robotic air war, complemented by cross-border helicopter attacks, CIA-funded "kill teams" of Afghan proxy forces, as well as boots-on-the-ground missions by elite special operations forces, including the SEAL raid that killed Osama bin Laden.

The CIA has conducted clandestine intelligence and surveillance missions in Pakistan, too, though its role may, in the future, be less important, thanks to Pentagon mission creep. In April 2012, in fact, Secretary of Defense Leon Panetta announced the creation of a new CIA-like espionage agency within the Pentagon called the Defense Clandestine Service. According to the *Washington Post*, its aim is to expand "the military's espionage efforts beyond war zones."

Over the last decade, the very notion of war zones has become remarkably muddled, mirroring the blurring of the missions and activities of the CIA and Pentagon. Analyzing the new agency and the "broader convergence trend" between Department of Defense and CIA missions, the *Post* noted that the "blurring is also evident in the organizations' upper ranks. Panetta previously served as CIA director, and that post is currently held by retired four-star Army Gen. David H. Petraeus."

Not to be outdone, the State Department, once the seat of diplomacy, continued on its long march to militarization (and marginalization) when it agreed to pool some of its resources with the Pentagon to create the Global Security Contingency Fund. That program will allow the Defense Department even greater say in how aid from Washington will flow to proxy forces in places like Yemen and the Horn of Africa.

One thing is certain: American war-making (along with its spies and its diplomats) is heading ever deeper into "the shadows." Expect yet more clandestine operations in ever more places with, of course, ever more potential for blowback in the years ahead.

Shedding Light on "the Dark Continent"

One locale likely to see an influx of Pentagon spies in the coming years is Africa. Under President Obama, operations on the continent have accelerated far beyond the more limited interventions of the Bush years. 2011's war in Libya; a regional drone campaign with missions run out of airports and bases in Djibouti, Ethiopia, and the Indian Ocean archipelago nation of Seychelles; a flotilla of 30 ships in that ocean supporting regional operations; a multi-pronged military and CIA campaign against militants in Somalia, including intelligence operations, training for Somali agents, a secret prison, helicopter attacks, and U.S. commando raids; a massive influx of cash for counterterrorism operations across East Africa; a possible old-fashioned air war, carried out on the sly in the region using manned aircraft; tens of millions of dollars in arms for allied mercenaries and African troops; and a special ops expeditionary force (bolstered by State Department experts) dispatched to help capture or kill Lord's Resistance Army leader Joseph Kony and his senior commanders, operating in Uganda, South Sudan, the Democratic Republic of the Congo, and the Central African Republic (where U.S. Special Forces now have a new base) only begins to scratch the surface of Washington's fast-expanding plans and activities in the region.

Even less well known are other U.S. military efforts designed to train African forces for operations now considered integral to American interests on the continent. These include, for example, a mission by elite Force Recon Marines from the Special Purpose Marine Air Ground Task Force 12 (SPMAGTF-12) to train soldiers from the Uganda People's Defense Force, which supplies the majority of troops to the African Union Mission in Somalia.

The U.S. is also conducting counterterrorism training and equipping militaries in Algeria, Burkina Faso, Chad, Mauritania,

Niger, and Tunisia. In addition, U.S. Africa Command (AFRICOM) has 14 major joint-training exercises planned for 2012, including operations in Morocco, Cameroon, Gabon, Botswana, South Africa, Lesotho, Senegal, and what may become the Pakistan of Africa, Nigeria.

Back in the Backyard

Since its founding, the United States has often meddled close to home, treating the Caribbean as its private lake and intervening at will throughout Latin America. During the Bush years, with some notable exceptions, Washington's interest in America's "backyard" took a backseat to wars farther from home. The Obama administration is now in the process of ramping up operations south of the border using its new formula. This has meant Pentagon drone missions deep inside Mexico to aid that country's battle against the drug cartels, while CIA agents and civilian operatives from the Department of Defense were dispatched to Mexican military bases to take part in the country's drug war.

In 2012, the Pentagon has also ramped up its anti-drug operations in Honduras. Working out of Forward Operating Base Mocoron and other remote camps there, the U.S. military is supporting Honduran operations by way of the methods it honed in Iraq and Afghanistan. In addition, Green Berets have been assisting Honduran Special Operations forces in anti-smuggling operations; and a Drug Enforcement Administration Foreign-deployed Advisory Support Team, originally created to disrupt the poppy trade in Afghanistan, has joined forces with Honduras's Tactical Response Team, that country's most elite counternarcotics unit. A glimpse of these operations made the news when DEA agents, flying in an American helicopter, were involved in an aerial attack on civilians that killed two men and two pregnant women in the remote Mosquito Coast region.

Less visible have been U.S. efforts in Guyana, where Special Operations Forces have been training local troops in heliborne air assault techniques. "This is the first time we have had this type of exercise involving Special Operations Forces of the United States on such a grand scale," Colonel Bruce Lovell of the Guyana Defense Force told a U.S. public affairs official. "It gives us a chance to validate ourselves and see where we are, what are our shortcomings."

Still in the Middle of the Middle East

Despite the end of the Iraq and Libyan wars, a coming drawdown of forces in Afghanistan, and copious public announcements about its national security pivot toward Asia, Washington is by no means withdrawing from the Greater Middle East. In addition to continuing operations in Afghanistan, the U.S. has consistently been at work training allied troops, building up military bases, and brokering weapons sales and arms transfers to despots in the region from Bahrain to Yemen.

In fact, Yemen, like its neighbor, Somalia, across the Gulf of Aden, has become a laboratory for Obama's wars. There, the U.S. is carrying out its signature new brand of warfare with "black ops" troops like the SEALs and the Army's Delta Force likely conducting kill/capture missions, while "white" forces like the Green Berets and Rangers are training indigenous troops, and robot planes hunt and kill members of al-Qaeda and its affiliates, possibly assisted by an even more secret contingent of manned aircraft.

The Middle East has also become the somewhat unlikely poster-region for another emerging facet of the Obama doctrine: cyberwar efforts. In a category-blurring speaking engagement,

Secretary of State Hillary Clinton surfaced at the 2012 Special Operations Forces Industry Conference in Florida where she gave a speech talking up her department's eagerness to join in the new American way of war. "We need Special Operations Forces who are as comfortable drinking tea with tribal leaders as raiding a terrorist compound," she told the crowd. "We also need diplomats and development experts who are up to the job of being your partners."

Clinton then took the opportunity to tout her agency's online efforts, aimed at websites used by al-Qaeda's affiliate in Yemen. When al-Qaeda recruitment messages appeared on the latter, she said, "our team plastered the same sites with altered versions… that showed the toll al-Qaeda attacks have taken on the Yemeni people." She further noted that this information-warfare mission was carried out by experts at the State Department's Center for Strategic Counterterrorism Communications with assistance, not surprisingly, from the military and the U.S. Intelligence Community.

These modest on-line efforts join more potent methods of cyberwar being employed by the Pentagon and the CIA, including "Olympic Games," a program of sophisticated attacks on computers in Iran's nuclear enrichment facilities engineered and unleashed by the National Security Agency (NSA) and Unit 8200, Israeli's equivalent of the NSA. As with other facets of the new way of war, these efforts were begun under the Bush administration but significantly accelerated under President Obama, who became the first American commander-in-chief to order sustained cyberattacks designed to cripple another country's infrastructure.

From Brushfires to Wildfires

Across the globe from Central and South America to Africa, the Middle East, and Asia, the Obama administration is working out its formula for a new American way of war. In its pursuit, the Pentagon and its increasingly militarized government partners are drawing on everything from classic precepts of colonial warfare to the latest technologies.

The United States is an imperial power chastened by more than 10 years of failed, heavy-footprint wars. It is hobbled by a hollowing-out economy, and inundated with hundreds of thousands of recent veterans — a staggering 45% of the troops who fought in Afghanistan and Iraq — suffering from service-related disabilities who will require ever more expensive care. No wonder the current combination of special ops, drones, spy games, civilian soldiers, cyberwarfare, and proxy fighters sounds like a safer, saner brand of war-fighting. At first blush, it may even look like a panacea for America's national security ills. In reality, it may be anything but.

The new light-footprint Obama doctrine actually seems to be making war an ever more attractive and seemingly easy option — a point emphasized by former Chairman of the Joint Chiefs of Staff General Peter Pace. "I worry about speed making it too easy to employ force," said Pace when asked about efforts to make it simpler to deploy Special Operations Forces abroad. "I worry about speed making it too easy to take the easy answer — let's go whack them with special operations — as opposed to perhaps a more laborious answer for perhaps a better long-term solution."

As a result, the new American way of war holds great potential for unforeseen entanglements and serial blowback. Starting or fanning brushfire wars on several continents could lead to raging wildfires that spread unpredictably and prove difficult, if not impossible, to quench.

By their very nature, small military engagements tend to get larger, and wars tend to spread beyond borders. By definition, military action tends to have unforeseen consequences. Those who doubt this need only look back to September 11, 2001, when three low-tech attacks on a single day set in motion a decade-plus of war that has spread across the globe. The response to that one day began with a war in Afghanistan, which spread to Pakistan, detoured to Iraq, popped up in Somalia and Yemen, and so on. Today, veterans of those Ur-interventions find themselves trying to replicate their dubious successes in places like Mexico and Honduras, the Central Africa Republic and the Congo.

History demonstrates that the U.S. is not very good at winning wars, having gone without victory in any major conflict since 1945. Smaller interventions have been a mixed bag with modest victories in places like Panama and Grenada and ignominious outcomes in Lebanon (in the 1980s) and Somalia (in the 1990s), to name a few.

The trouble is, it's hard to tell what an intervention will grow up to be — until it's too late. While they followed different paths, Vietnam, Afghanistan, and Iraq all began relatively small, before growing large and ruinous. Already, the outlook for the new Obama doctrine seems far from rosy, despite the good press it's getting inside Washington's Beltway.

What looks today like a formula for easy power projection that will further U.S. imperial interests on the cheap could soon prove to be an unmitigated disaster — one that likely won't be apparent until it's too late.

2.

Uncovering the Military's
Secret Military

Somewhere on this planet an American commando is carrying out a mission. Now, say that 70 times and you're done... for the day. Without the knowledge of the American public, a secret force within the U.S. military is undertaking operations in a majority of the world's countries. This new Pentagon power elite is waging a global war whose size and scope have never been revealed, until now.

After a U.S. Navy SEAL put a bullet in Osama bin Laden's chest and another in his head, one of the most secretive black-ops units in the American military suddenly found its mission in the public spotlight. It was atypical. While it's well known that U.S. Special Operations forces are deployed in the war zones of Afghanistan and Iraq, and it's increasingly apparent that such units operate in murkier conflict zones like Yemen and Somalia, the full extent of their worldwide war has remained deeply in the shadows.

In 2010, Karen DeYoung and Greg Jaffe of the *Washington Post* reported that U.S. Special Operations Forces were deployed in 75 countries, up from 60 at the end of the Bush presidency. By the end of 2011, U.S. Special Operations Command spokesman Colonel Tim Nye told me, that number would reach 120. "We do a lot of traveling — a lot more than Afghanistan or Iraq," he said. This global presence — in about 60% of the world's nations and far larger than previously acknowledged — provides striking new evidence of a rising clandestine Pentagon power elite waging a secret war in all corners of the world.

The Rise of the Military's Secret Military

Born of a failed 1980 raid to rescue American hostages in Iran, in which eight U.S. service members died, U.S. Special Operations Command (SOCOM) was established in 1987. Having spent the post-Vietnam years distrusted and starved for money by the regular military, special operations forces suddenly had a single home, a stable budget, and a four-star commander as their advocate. Since then, SOCOM has grown into a combined force of startling proportions. Made up of units from all the service branches, including the Army's Green Berets and Rangers, Navy SEALs, Air Force Air Commandos, and Marine Corps Special Operations teams, in addition to specialized helicopter crews, boat teams, civil affairs personnel, para-rescuemen, and even battlefield air-traffic controllers and special operations weathermen, SOCOM carries out the United States' most specialized and secret missions. These include assassinations, counterterrorist raids, long-range reconnaissance, intelligence analysis, foreign troop training, and weapons of mass destruction counter-proliferation operations.

One of its key components is the Joint Special Operations

Command, or JSOC, a clandestine sub-command whose primary mission is tracking and killing suspected terrorists. Reporting to the president and acting under his authority, JSOC maintains a global hit list that includes American citizens. It has been operating an extra-legal "kill/capture" campaign that John Nagl, a past counterinsurgency adviser to former four-star general and now CIA Director David Petraeus, calls "an almost industrial-scale counterterrorism killing machine."

This assassination program has been carried out by commando units like the Navy SEALs and the Army's Delta Force as well as via drone strikes as part of covert wars in which the CIA is also involved in countries like Somalia, Pakistan, and Yemen. In addition, the command operates a network of secret prisons, perhaps as many as 20 black sites in Afghanistan alone, used for interrogating high-value targets.

Growth Industry

From a force of about 37,000 in the early 1990s, Special Operations Command personnel have grown to almost 60,000, about a third of whom are career members of SOCOM; the rest have other military occupational specialties, but periodically cycle through the command. Growth has been exponential since September 11, 2001, as SOCOM's baseline budget almost tripled from $2.3 billion to $6.3 billion. If you add in funding for the wars in Iraq and Afghanistan, it has actually more than quadrupled to $9.8 billion in these years. Not surprisingly, the number of its personnel deployed abroad has also jumped four-fold. Further increases, and expanded operations, are on the horizon.

Lieutenant General Dennis Hejlik, the former head of the Marine Corps Forces Special Operations Command — the last of the service branches to be incorporated into SOCOM in 2006 — indicated, for instance, that he foresees a doubling of his former unit of 2,600. "I see them as a force someday of about 5,000, like equivalent to the number of SEALs that we have on the battlefield. Between [5,000] and 6,000," he said at a June 2012 breakfast with defense reporters in Washington. Long-term plans already call for the force to increase by 1,000.

During his Senate confirmation hearings, Navy Vice Admiral William McRaven, the incoming SOCOM chief and outgoing head of JSOC (which he commanded during the bin Laden raid) endorsed a steady manpower growth rate of 3% to 5% a year, while also making a pitch for even more resources, including additional drones and the construction of new special operations facilities.

A former SEAL, McRaven expressed a belief that, as conventional forces are drawn down in Afghanistan, special ops troops will take on an ever greater role. He also assured the Senate Armed Services Committee that "as a former JSOC commander, I can tell you we were looking very hard at Yemen and at Somalia."

During a speech at the 2011 National Defense Industrial Association's annual Special Operations and Low-Intensity Conflict Symposium, Navy Admiral Eric Olson, the outgoing chief of Special Operations Command, pointed to a composite satellite image of the world at night. Before September 11, 2001, the lit portions of the planet — mostly the industrialized nations of the global north — were considered the key areas. "But the world changed over the last decade," he said. "Our strategic focus has shifted largely to the south... certainly within the special operations community, as we deal with the emerging threats from the places where the lights aren't."

To that end, Olson launched "Project Lawrence," an effort to increase cultural proficiencies — like advanced language training and better knowledge of local history and customs — for overseas operations. The program is, of course, named after the British officer, Thomas Edward Lawrence (better known as "Lawrence of Arabia"), who teamed up with Arab fighters to wage a guerrilla war in the Middle East during World War I. Mentioning Afghanistan, Pakistan, Mali, and Indonesia, Olson added that SOCOM now needed "Lawrences of Wherever."

While Olson made reference to only 51 countries of top concern to SOCOM, Col. Nye told me that on any given day, Special Operations forces are deployed in approximately 70 nations around the world. All of them, he hastened to add, at the request of the host government. According to testimony by Olson before the House Armed Services Committee, approximately 85% of special operations troops deployed overseas are in 20 countries in the CENT-COM area of operations in the Greater Middle East: Afghanistan, Bahrain, Egypt, Iran, Iraq, Jordan, Kazakhstan, Kuwait, Kyrgyzstan, Lebanon, Oman, Pakistan, Qatar, Saudi Arabia, Syria, Tajikistan, Turkmenistan, United Arab Emirates, Uzbekistan, and Yemen. The others are scattered across the globe from South America to Southeast Asia, some in small numbers, others as larger contingents.

Special Operations Command won't disclose exactly which countries its forces operate in. "We're obviously going to have some places where it's not advantageous for us to list where we're at," says Nye. "Not all host nations want it known, for whatever reasons they have — it may be internal, it may be regional."

But it's no secret (or at least a poorly kept one) that so-called black special operations troops, like the SEALs and Delta Force, are conducting kill/capture missions in Afghanistan, Pakistan, and Yemen, while "white" forces like the Green Berets and Rangers are training indigenous partners as part of a worldwide secret war against al-Qaeda and other militant groups. In the Philippines, for instance, the U.S. spends $50 million a year on a 600-person contingent of Army Special Operations forces, Navy Seals, Air Force special operators, and others that carries out counterterrorist operations with Filipino allies against insurgent groups like Jemaah Islamiyah and Abu Sayyaf.

In 2010, as an analysis of SOCOM documents, open-source Pentagon information, and a database of Special Operations missions compiled by investigative journalist Tara McKelvey (for the Medill School of Journalism's National Security Journalism Initiative) reveals, America's most elite troops carried out joint training exercises in Belize, Brazil, Bulgaria, Burkina Faso, Germany, Indonesia, Mali, Norway, Panama, and Poland. In 2011, similar training missions were conducted in the Dominican Republic, Jordan, Romania, Senegal, South Korea, and Thailand, among other nations. In reality, Nye told me, training actually went on in almost every nation where Special Operations forces are deployed. "Of the 120 countries we visit by the end of the year, I would say the vast majority are training exercises in one fashion or another. They would be classified as training exercises."

The Pentagon's Power Elite

Once the neglected stepchildren of the military establishment, Special Operations forces have been growing exponentially not just in size and budget, but also in power and influence. Since 2002, SOCOM has been authorized to create its own Joint Task Forces — like Joint Special Operations Task Force-Philippines — a prerogative normally limited to larger combatant commands like CENTCOM. In 2011, without much fanfare, SOCOM also established its own Joint Acquisition Task Force, a cadre of equipment designers and acquisition specialists.

With control over budgeting, training, and equipping its force, powers usually reserved for departments (like the Department of the Army or the Department of the Navy), dedicated dollars in every Defense Department budget, and influential advocates in Congress, SOCOM is by now an exceptionally powerful player at the Pentagon. With real clout, it can win bureaucratic battles, purchase cutting-edge technology, and pursue fringe research like electronically beaming messages into people's heads or developing stealth cloaking technologies for ground troops. Since 2001, SOCOM's prime contracts awarded to small businesses — those that generally produce specialty equipment and weapons — have jumped six-fold.

Headquartered at MacDill Air Force Base in Florida, but operating out of theater commands spread around the globe, including Hawaii, Germany, and South Korea, and active in the majority of countries on the planet, Special Operations Command is now a force unto itself. As outgoing SOCOM chief Olson put it, SOCOM "is a microcosm of the Department of Defense, with ground, air, and maritime components, a global presence, and authorities and responsibilities that mirror the Military Departments, Military Services, and Defense Agencies."

Tasked to coordinate all Pentagon planning against global terrorism networks and, as a result, closely connected to other government agencies, foreign militaries, and intelligence services, and armed with a vast inventory of stealthy helicopters, manned fixed-wing aircraft, heavily armed drones, high-tech guns-a-go-go speedboats, specialized Humvees, and Mine Resistant Ambush Protected vehicles, or MRAPs, as well as other state-of-the-art gear (with more on the way), SOCOM represents something new in the military. Whereas the late scholar of militarism Chalmers Johnson used to refer to the CIA as "the president's private army," today

JSOC performs that role, acting as the chief executive's private assassination squad, and its parent, SOCOM, functions as a new Pentagon power-elite, a secret military within the military possessing domestic power and global reach.

In 120 countries across the globe, troops from Special Operations Command carry out their secret war of high-profile assassinations, low-level targeted killings, capture/kidnap operations, kick-down-the-door night raids, joint operations with foreign forces, and training missions with indigenous partners as part of a shadowy conflict unknown to most Americans. Once "special" for being small, lean, outsider outfits, today they are special for their power, access, influence, and aura.

That aura now benefits from a well-honed public relations campaign which helps them project a superhuman image at home and abroad, even while many of their actual activities remain in the ever-widening shadows. Typical of the vision they are pushing was this statement from Admiral Olson: "I am convinced that the forces... are the most culturally attuned partners, the most lethal hunter-killers, and most responsive, agile, innovative, and efficiently effective advisors, trainers, problem-solvers, and warriors that any nation has to offer."

At the Aspen Institute's 2011 Security Forum, Olson offered up similarly gilded comments and some misleading information, too, claiming that U.S. Special Operations forces were operating in just 65 countries and engaged in combat in only two of them. When asked about drone strikes in Pakistan, he reportedly replied, "Are you talking about unattributed explosions?"

What he did let slip, however, was telling. He noted, for instance, that black operations like the bin Laden mission, with commandos conducting heliborne night raids, were now exceptionally common. A dozen or so are conducted every night, he said. Perhaps most illuminating was an offhand remark about the size of SOCOM. Right now, he emphasized, U.S. Special Operations forces were approximately as large as Canada's entire active duty military. In fact, the force is larger than the active duty militaries of many of the nations where America's elite troops now operate each year, and it's only set to grow larger.

Americans have yet to grapple with what it means to have a "special" force this large, this active, and this secret — and they are unlikely to begin to do so until more information is available. It just won't be coming from Olson or his troops. "Our access [to foreign countries] depends on our ability to not talk about it," he said in response to questions about SOCOM's secrecy. When missions are subject to scrutiny like the bin Laden raid, he said, the elite troops object. The military's secret military, said Olson, wants "to get back into the shadows and do what they came in to do."

3.

America's Empire of Drone Bases

They increasingly dot the planet. There's a facility outside Las Vegas where "pilots" work in climate-controlled trailers, another at a dusty camp in Africa formerly used by the French Foreign Legion, a third at a big air base in Afghanistan where Air Force personnel sit in front of multiple computer screens, and a fourth at an air base in the United Arab Emirates that almost no one talks about.

And that leaves at least 56 more such facilities to mention in an expanding American empire of unmanned drone bases being set up worldwide. Despite frequent news reports on the drone assassination campaigns launched in support of America's ever-widening undeclared wars and a spate of stories on drone bases in Africa and the Middle East, most of these facilities have remained unnoted, uncounted, and remarkably anonymous — until now.

Run by the military, the Central Intelligence Agency, and their proxies, these bases — some little more than desolate airstrips, others sophisticated command and control centers filled with computer screens and high-tech electronic equipment — are the backbone of a new American robotic way of war. They are also the latest development in a long-evolving saga of American power projection abroad; in this case, remote-controlled strikes anywhere on the planet with a minimal foreign "footprint" and little accountability.

Using military documents, press accounts, and other open source information, an in-depth analysis by TomDispatch has identified at least 60 bases integral to U.S. military and CIA drone operations. There may, however, be more, since a cloak of secrecy about drone warfare leaves the full size and scope of these bases distinctly in the shadows. (In 2012, it was revealed that the Department of Defense has identified 110 potential bases for drone operations at military installations in the United States alone.)

A Galaxy of Bases

Over the last decade, the American use of unmanned aerial vehicles (UAVs) and unmanned aerial systems (UAS) has expanded exponentially, as has media coverage of their use. On September 21, 2011, the *Wall Street Journal* reported that the military had deployed missile-armed MQ-9 Reaper drones to the "island nation of Seychelles to intensify attacks on al Qaeda affiliates, particularly in Somalia." A day earlier, a *Washington Post* piece also mentioned the same base on the tiny Indian Ocean archipelago, as well as one in the African nation of Djibouti, another under construction in Ethiopia, and a secret CIA airstrip being built for drones in an unnamed Middle Eastern country. (Some suspect it's Saudi Arabia.)

Post journalists Greg Miller and Craig Whitlock reported that the "Obama administration is assembling a constellation of secret drone bases for counterterrorism operations in the Horn of Africa and the Arabian Peninsula as part of a newly aggressive campaign to attack al-Qaeda affiliates in Somalia and Yemen." Within days, the *Post* also reported that a drone from the new CIA base in that unidentified Middle Eastern country had carried out the assassination of radical al-Qaeda preacher and American citizen Anwar al-Awlaki in Yemen.

With the killing of al-Awlaki, the Obama administration had expanded its armed drone campaign to no fewer than six countries, though the CIA, which killed al-Awlaki, refuses to officially acknowledge its drone assassination program. The Air Force is less coy about its drone operations, yet there are many aspects of those, too, that remain in the shadows. Air Force spokesman Lieutenant Colonel John Haynes told TomDispatch that, "for operational security reasons, we do not discuss worldwide operating locations of Remotely Piloted Aircraft, to include numbers of locations around the world."

Still, those 60 military and CIA bases worldwide directly connected to the drone program tell us much about America's war-making future. From command and control and piloting to maintenance and arming, these facilities perform key functions that allow drone campaigns to continue expanding, as they have for more than a decade. Other bases are already under construction or in the planning stages. When presented with our list of Air Force sites within America's galaxy of drone bases, Lieutenant Colonel Haynes responded, "I have nothing further to add to what I've already said."

Even in the face of government secrecy, however, much can be discovered. Here, then, for the record is a TomDispatch accounting of America's drone bases in the United States and around the world.

The Near Abroad

News reports have frequently focused on Creech Air Force Base outside Las Vegas as ground zero in America's military drone campaign. Sitting in darkened, air-conditioned rooms 7,500 miles from Afghanistan, drone pilots dressed in flight suits remotely control MQ-9 Reapers and their progenitors, the less heavily-armed MQ-1 Predators. Beside them, sensor operators manipulate the TV camera, infrared camera, and other high-tech sensors on board the plane. Their faces are lit up by digital displays showing video feeds from the battle zone. By squeezing a trigger on a joystick, one of those Air Force "pilots" can loose a Hellfire missile on a person half a world away.

While Creech gets the lion's share of media attention — it even has its own drones on site — numerous other bases on U.S. soil have played critical roles in America's drone wars. The same video-game-style warfare is carried out by U.S. and British pilots not far away at Nevada's Nellis Air Force Base, the home of the Air Force's 2nd Special Operations Squadron (SOS). According to a factsheet provided to TomDispatch by the Air Force, the 2nd SOS and its drone operators are scheduled to be relocated to the Air Force Special Operations Command at Hurlburt Field in Florida.

Reapers or Predators are also being flown from Davis-Monthan Air Force Base in Arizona, Whiteman Air Force Base in Missouri, March Air Reserve Base in California, Springfield Air National Guard Base in Ohio, Cannon Air Force Base and Holloman Air Force Base in New Mexico, Ellington Airport in Houston, Texas, the Air National Guard base in Fargo, North Dakota, Ellsworth Air Force Base in South Dakota, and Hancock Field Air National Guard Base in Syracuse, New York. In 2011, it was announced that Reapers flown by Hancock's pilots would begin taking off on training missions from the Army's Fort Drum, also in New York State.

Meanwhile, at Langley Air Force Base in Virginia, according to a report by the *New York Times*, teams of camouflage-clad Air Force analysts sit in a secret intelligence and surveillance installation monitoring cell-phone intercepts, high-altitude photographs, and most notably, multiple screens of streaming live video from drones in Afghanistan. They call it "Death TV" and are constantly instant-messaging with and talking to commanders on the ground in order to supply them with real-time intelligence on enemy troop movements. Air Force analysts also closely monitor the battlefield from Air Force Special Operations Command in Florida and a facility in Terre Haute, Indiana.

CIA drone operators also reportedly pilot their aircraft from the Agency's nearby Langley, Virginia headquarters. It was from here that analysts apparently watched footage of Osama bin Laden's compound in Pakistan, for example, thanks to video sent back by the RQ-170 Sentinel, an advanced drone nicknamed the "Beast of Kandahar." According to Air Force documents, the Sentinel is flown from both Creech Air Force Base and Tonopah Test Range in Nevada.

Predators, Reapers, and Sentinels are just part of the story. At Beale Air Force Base in California, Air Force personnel pilot RQ-4 Global Hawks, unmanned drones used for long-range, high-altitude surveillance missions, some of them originating from Anderson Air Force Base in Guam (a staging ground for drone flights over Asia). Other Global Hawks are stationed at Grand Forks Air Force Base in North Dakota, while the Aeronautical Systems Center at Wright-Patterson Air Force Base in Ohio manages the Global Hawk as well as the Predator and Reaper programs for the Air Force.

Other bases have been intimately involved in training drone operators, including Randolph Air Force Base in Texas and New

Mexico's Kirtland Air Force Base, as has the Army's Fort Huachuca in Arizona, which is home to "the world's largest UAV training center," according to a report by *National Defense* magazine. There, hundreds of employees of defense giant General Dynamics train military personnel to fly smaller tactical drones like the Hunter and the Shadow. The physical testing of drones goes on at adjoining Libby Army Airfield and "two UAV runways located approximately four miles west of Libby," according to Global Security, an on-line clearinghouse for military information.

Additionally, small drone training for the Army is carried out at Fort Benning in Georgia while at Fort Rucker, Alabama — "the home of Army aviation" — the Unmanned Aircraft Systems program coordinates doctrine, strategy, and concepts pertaining to UAVs. Fort Benning also saw the early testing of true robotic drones — which fly without human guidance or a hand on any joystick. This, wrote the *Washington Post*, is considered the next step toward a future in which drones will "hunt, identify, and kill the enemy based on calculations made by software, not decisions made by humans."

The Army has also carried out UAV training exercises at Dugway Proving Ground in Utah and the Navy launched its X-47B, a next-generation semi-autonomous stealth drone, on its first flight at Edwards Air Force Base in California. Designed to operate from the decks of aircraft carriers, that flying robot was then sent on to Maryland's Naval Air Station Patuxent River for further testing. At nearby Webster Field, the Navy worked out kinks in its Fire Scout pilotless helicopter, which has also been tested at Fort Rucker and Yuma Proving Ground in Arizona, as well as Florida's Mayport Naval Station and Jacksonville Naval Air Station. The latter base was also where the Navy's Broad Area Maritime Surveillance (BAMS) unmanned aerial system was developed. It is now based there and at Naval Air Station Whidbey Island in Washington State.

Foreign Jewels in the Crown

The Navy is actively looking for a suitable site in the Western Pacific for a BAMS base, and is currently in talks with several Persian Gulf states about a site in the Middle East. It already has Global Hawks perched at its base in Sigonella, Italy.

The Air Force negotiated with Turkey to relocate some of the Predator drones that operated in Iraq to the giant air base at Incirlik. Many different UAVs had been based in Iraq following the American invasion of that country, including small tactical models like the Raven-B that troops launched by hand from Kirkuk Regional Air Base, Shadow UAVs that flew from Forward Operating Base Normandy in Baqubah Province, Predators operating out of Balad Airbase, miniature Desert Hawk drones launched from Tallil Air Base, and Scan Eagles based at Al Asad Air Base.

Elsewhere in the Greater Middle East, according to *Aviation Week*, the military is launching Global Hawks from Al Dhafra Air Base in the United Arab Emirates, piloted by personnel stationed at Naval Air Station Patuxent River in Maryland, to track "shipping traffic in the Persian Gulf, Strait of Hormuz, and Arabian Sea." There are unconfirmed reports that the CIA may be operating drones from the Emirates as well. In the past, other UAVs have apparently been flown from Kuwait's Ali Al Salem Air Base and Al Jaber Air Base, as well as Seeb Air Base in Oman.

At Al-Udeid Air Base in Qatar, the Air Force runs an air operations command and control facility, critical to the drone wars in Afghanistan and Pakistan. The new secret CIA base on the Arabian peninsula, used to assassinate Anwar al-Awlaki, may or may not be the airstrip in Saudi Arabia whose existence a senior U.S. military official confirmed to Fox News. In the past, the CIA has also operated UAVs out of Tuzel, Uzbekistan.

In neighboring Afghanistan, drones fly from many bases including Jalalabad Air Base, Kandahar Air Field, the air base at Bagram, Camp Leatherneck, Camp Dwyer, Combat Outpost Payne, Forward Operating Base (FOB) Edinburgh and FOB Delaram II, to name a few. Afghan bases are, however, more than just locations where drones take off and land.

It is a common misconception that U.S.-based operators are the only ones who "fly" America's armed drones. In fact, in and around America's war zones, UAVs begin and end their flights under the control of local "pilots." Take Afghanistan's massive Bagram Air Base. After performing preflight checks alongside a technician who focuses on the drone's sensors, a local airman sits in front of a Dell computer tower and multiple monitors, two keyboards, a joystick, a throttle, a rollerball, a mouse, and various switches, overseeing the plane's takeoff before handing it over to a stateside counterpart with a similar electronics set-up. After the mission is complete, the controls are transferred back to the local operators for the landing. Additionally, crews in Afghanistan perform general maintenance and repairs on the drones.

In the wake of a devastating suicide attack by an al-Qaeda double agent that killed CIA officers and contractors at Forward Operating Base Chapman in Afghanistan's eastern province of Khost in 2009, it came to light that the facility was heavily involved in target selection for drone strikes across the border in Pakistan. The drones themselves, as the *Washington Post* noted at the time, were "flown from separate bases in Afghanistan and Pakistan."

Both the Air Force and the CIA have conducted operations in Pakistani air space, with some missions originating in Afghanistan and others from inside Pakistan. In 2006, images of what appear to be Predator drones stationed at Shamsi Air Base in Pakistan's Balochistan province were found on Google Earth and later published. In 2009, the *New York Times* reported that operatives from Xe Services, the company formerly known as Blackwater, had taken over the task of arming Predator drones at the CIA's "hidden bases in Pakistan and Afghanistan."

Following the May 2011 Navy SEAL raid into Pakistan that killed Osama bin Laden, that country's leaders reportedly ordered the United States to leave Shamsi. The base, according to the *Washington Post*, was actually owned and sublet to the U.S. by the United Arab Emirates, which had built the airfield "as an arrival point for falconry and other hunting expeditions in Pakistan."

The U.S. and Pakistani governments have since claimed that Shamsi is no longer being used for drone strikes. True or not, the U.S. evidently also uses other Pakistani bases for its drones, including possibly PAF Base Shahbaz, located near the city of Jacobabad, and another base located near Ghazi.

The New Scramble for Africa

More recently, the headline story, when it comes to the expansion of the empire of drone bases, has been Africa. For the last decade, the U.S. military has been operating out of Camp Lemonier, a former French Foreign Legion base in the tiny African nation of Djibouti. Not long after the attacks of September 11, 2001, it became a base for Predator drones and has since been used to conduct missions over neighboring Somalia.

For some time, rumors have also been circulating about a secret American base in Ethiopia. In 2011, a U.S. official revealed to the *Washington Post* that discussions about a drone base there had been underway for up to four years, "but that plan was delayed because 'the Ethiopians were not all that jazzed.'" Now construction is evidently complete.

Then, of course, there is that base on the Seychelles in the Indian Ocean. A small fleet of Navy and Air Force drones began operating openly there in 2009 to track pirates in the region's waters. Classified diplomatic cables obtained by Wikileaks, however, reveal that those drones have also secretly been used to carry out missions in Somalia. "Based in a hangar located about a quarter-mile from the main passenger terminal at the airport," the *Post* reports, the base consists of three or four "Reapers and about 100 U.S. military personnel and contractors, according to the cables."

The U.S. also sent four smaller tactical drones to the African nations of Uganda and Burundi for use by their militaries.

New and Old Empires

Even if the Pentagon budget were to begin to shrink, expansion of America's empire of drone bases is a sure thing in the years to come. Drones are now the bedrock of Washington's future military planning and — with counterinsurgency out of favor — one of the preferred ways of carrying out attacks abroad.

During the eight years of George W. Bush's presidency, as the U.S. was building up its drone fleets, the country launched wars in Afghanistan and Iraq, and carried out limited strikes in Yemen, Pakistan, and Somalia, using drones in at least four of those countries. In less than three years under President Obama, the U.S. launched drone strikes in Afghanistan, Iraq, Libya, Pakistan, Somalia, and Yemen. It maintains that it has carte blanche to kill suspected enemies in any nation (or at least any nation in the global south).

According to a 2011 report by the Congressional Budget Office, "the Department of Defense plans to purchase about 730 new medium-sized and large unmanned aircraft systems" over the next decade. In practical terms, this means more drones like the Reaper.

Military officials told the *Wall Street Journal* that the Reaper "can fly 1,150 miles from base, conduct missions, and return home… [T]he time a drone can stay aloft depends on how heavily armed it is." According to a drone operator training document obtained by TomDispatch, at maximum payload, meaning with 3,750 pounds worth of Hellfire missiles and GBU-12 or GBU-30 bombs on board, the Reaper can remain aloft for 16 to 20 hours.

Even a glance at a world map tells you that, if the U.S. is to carry out ever more drone strikes across the developing world, it will need more bases for its future UAVs. As an unnamed senior military official pointed out to a *Washington Post* reporter, speaking of all those new drone bases clustered around the Somali and Yemeni war zones, "If you look at it geographically, it makes sense — you get out a ruler and draw the distances [drones] can fly and where they take off from."

An analysis by TomDispatch determined that there were more than 1,000 U.S. military bases scattered across the globe — a shadowy base-world providing plenty of existing sites that can, and no doubt will, host drones. But facilities selected for a pre-drone world may not always prove optimal locations for America's current and future undeclared wars and assassination campaigns. So further expansion in Africa, the Middle East, and Asia is likely.

What are the Air Force's plans in this regard? Lieutenant Colonel John Haynes was typically circumspect, saying, "We are constantly evaluating potential operating locations based on evolving mission needs." If the last decade is any indication, those "needs" will only continue to grow.

4.

Arming Mideast Autocrats

If you follow the words, one Middle East comes into view; if you follow the weapons, quite another.

In May 2011, President Obama announced a reset of American policy in the Middle East with a major address offering a comprehensive look at the Arab Spring, "a unified theory about the popular uprisings from Tunisia to Bahrain," and a new administration approach to the region.

At the same time, all signs indicated that the Pentagon would quietly maintain antithetical policies, just as it had throughout the Obama years. Barring an unprecedented and almost inconceivable policy shift, it will continue to broker lucrative deals to send weapons systems and military equipment to Arab despots. Nothing indicates that it will be deterred from its course, whatever the president says, which means that Barack Obama's reset rhetoric is unlikely to translate into meaningful policy change in the region.

For months, the world watched as protesters took to the streets across the Middle East to demand a greater say in their lives. In Tunisia and Egypt, they toppled decades-old dictatorships. In Bahrain and Yemen, they were shot down in the streets as they demanded democracy. In the United Arab Emirates, Kuwait, Jordan and Saudi Arabia, they called for reforms, free speech, and basic rights, and ended up bloodied and often in jail cells. In Iraq, they protested a lack of food and jobs, and in response got bullets and beatings.

As the world watched, trained eyes couldn't help noticing something startling about the tools of repression in those countries. The armored personnel carriers, tanks, and helicopters used to intimidate or even kill peaceful protesters were often American models.

For decades, the U.S. has provided military aid, facilitated the sale of weaponry, and transferred vast quantities of arms to a host of Middle Eastern despots. Arming Arab autocrats, however, isn't only the work of presidents past. A TomDispatch analysis of Pentagon documents finds that the Obama administration has sought to send billions of dollars in weapons systems — from advanced helicopters to fighter jets — to the very regimes that have beaten, jailed, and killed pro-democracy demonstrators, journalists, and reform activists throughout the Arab Spring.

The administration's abiding support for the militaries of repressive regimes has called into question the president's rhetoric about change. The arms deals of recent years have also shed light on the shadowy, mutually supportive relationships among the U.S. military, top arms dealers, and Arab states that are of increasing importance to the Pentagon.

Since the summer of 2009, President Obama, by way of the Pentagon and with State Department approval, regularly notified Congress of his intent to sell advanced weaponry to governments across the Middle East, including Bahrain, Egypt, Iraq, Jordan, Kuwait, Saudi Arabia, Tunisia, and the United Arab Emirates (UAE). Under U.S. law, Congress has 30 days to review the sale before the Pentagon and associated military contractors enter into more formal contract talks with individual nations.

In July 2009, according to an analysis of Pentagon documents by TomDispatch, notifications were sent to Congress regarding the sale to Kuwait of Browning machine guns, advanced targeting systems for armored vehicles, KC-130 aircraft, and technical support for F/A-18 attack aircraft. Later that summer, the White House announced plans to outfit both Bahrain's and Jordan's militaries with advanced air-to-air missiles to the tune of $74 million and $131 million, respectively, to equip the United Arab Emirates with $526 million worth of Hellfire missiles and other materiel, to send more than $2 billion worth of advanced surveillance and navigation equipment to aid Saudi Arabia's air force, and to see to it that Egypt's military received a shipment of new Chinook troop transport helicopters and other high-tech equipment valued at $308 million.

In the fall of 2009, Pentagon documents show a $220 million bid by the administration to outfit the Jordanian military with advanced rocket systems and tactical vehicles, a proposed sale of advanced fighter aircraft, parts, weapons, and equipment to Egypt worth as much as $3.2 billion, and another to equip Kuwait's military with $410 million in Patriot missile technology. Then, in November and December of that year, Congress was notified of plans to sell helicopters to Iraq, Javelin guided missiles to Jordan, Hellfire missiles, anti-ship cruise missiles, jet engines, and other military materiel to Egypt, and helicopters and thousands of advanced bombs, among other high-tech equipment, to the UAE.

In 2010, notifications also went out concerning the sale of F-16 fighters, armored personnel carriers, tank ammunition, and advanced computer systems to Iraq, C-17 military transport aircraft for Kuwait, mobile missile systems for Bahrain, and Apache attack helicopters and tactical missile systems for the United Arab Emirates. Saudi Arabia, however, was the big winner by far with a blockbuster $60 billion agreement for helicopters, fighter jets, radar equipment, and advanced smart bombs that will represent, if all purchases are made, the largest foreign arms deal in American history.

Deficits, Ducats, and Dictators

The agreement to broker the sale of tens of billions of dollars worth of weapons to Saudi Arabia sheds light on the Pentagon's efforts to shield itself — and its favored arms dealers — from the shakiness of the American economy, as well as President Obama's stated goal of trimming $400 billion from projected national security spending of $10 trillion over the next 12 years. In October 2010, the Pentagon started secretly lobbying financial analysts and large institutional investors on behalf of weapons makers and other military contractors. The idea was to bolster their long-term financial viability in the face of a possible future slowdown in Defense Department spending.

Then Deputy Secretary of Defense William Lynn and other Pentagon powerbrokers made regular trips to New York City to shore up Wall Street's support for weapons manufacturers. "We are in this for the long term. We need industrial partners and financial backers who think and act likewise," Lynn told investors at a defense and aerospace conference in that city.

Along with Ashton Carter, the Pentagon's undersecretary of defense for acquisition, technology, and logistics, and Brett Lambert, the deputy assistant secretary for industrial policy, Lynn created a comprehensive plan to sustain and enrich weapons makers and other military contractors in the coming years. "We're going sector by sector, tier by tier, and our goal is to develop a long-term policy to protect that base as we slow defense spending," Lynn said. America's Middle Eastern allies are seen as a significant partner in this effort.

It's often said that the Pentagon is a "monopsony" — that is, the only buyer in town for its many giant contractors. As has been amply demonstrated since Barack Obama took office, however, it's not true. When it comes to the Middle East, the Pentagon acts not as a buyer, but as a broker and shill, clearing the way for its Middle Eastern partners to buy some of the world's most advanced weaponry.

And Arab allies have distinctly done their part for the Pentagon. From 2006 to 2009, according to a report by the Congressional Research Service (CRS), the United States accounted for 52.4% of all arms agreements inked with Middle Eastern nations — to the tune of $47.3 billion. (By comparison, the United Kingdom, in second place in arms sales in the region, accounted for only 15.7% and third-place Russia just 12.8%. A separate CRS report would later reveal that in 2011, overseas weapons sales by the United States totaled $66.3 billion or almost 78% of the global arms market, much of it driven by sales to Persian Gulf nations. Russia was a distant second, with just $4.8 billion in total sales.)

The purchases of the chief buyer in the Middle East, Saudi Arabia, have been climbing steadily. From 2002 to 2005, Saudi Arabia inked $15.3 billion in arms-transfer agreements with the United States. From 2006 to 2009, that figure jumped to $29.5 billion. The multi-year $60 billion deal in 2010 signaled far more of the same and will help ensure the continuing health and profitability of Boeing, Lockheed-Martin, and other mega-defense contractors even if Pentagon spending goes slack or begins to shrink in the years to come.

The Pentagon's reliance on the deep pockets of Arab partners across the Middle East, however, has a price, which may help to explain the Obama administration's willingness to support dictators like Tunisia's Zine El Abidine Ben Ali and Egypt's Hosni Mubarak until their ousters were givens, and to essentially look the other way as security forces in Bahrain, Saudi Arabia, and elsewhere, sometimes using American-supplied equipment, suppressed pro-democracy activists. After all, the six member states of the Gulf Cooperation Council — Bahrain, Kuwait, Oman, Qatar, Saudi Arabia, and the UAE, along with regional partner Jordan — were slated to spend $70 billion on American weaponry and equipment in 2011 and as much as $80 billion per year by 2015.

"The Middle East Military Air Market: Revenue Opportunities and Stakeholder Mapping," a recent analysis of just one sector of defense spending in the region by U.S.-based defense consultants Frost and Sullivan, projects yet more growth in the future. "[The] regional military air market is... set to generate revenues of $62.9 billion between 2010 and 2020," it reports. Frost and Sullivan analysts add that Saudi Arabia and the United Arab Emirates are likely to be the biggest spenders and will continue to buy most of their arms through the United States for the sake of "political influence."

For his part, Lynn sought to make it ever easier to put sophisticated military technology in the hands of such deep-pocketed allies. On a trip to New York, he spoke of streamlining the process by which tanks, jets, and other advanced weapons systems are sold around the world. "To keep our base healthy, it is in our interest for defense companies to compete globally," he explained, while deriding the current system for selling arms abroad as "archaic" and in need of an overhaul. "The barriers that we place at this point in the export control system look something like a marriage of the complexity of the Internal Revenue Service with the efficiency of the Department of Motor Vehicles," he said. "It's something we have to change."

Sending a Message

In February 2011, in Baghdad, Fallujah, Mosul, and Tikrit, Iraqi protesters took to the streets, focused on ending corruption and chronic shortages of food, water, electricity, and jobs. In response, Prime Minister Nouri al-Maliki, who was consolidating power with U.S. military backing, unleashed government security forces. They arrested, beat, and shot protesters, leaving hundreds dead or wounded. Afterward, the Obama administration not only failed to forcefully rebuke the Maliki regime, but announced its intent to bolster those same security forces with another $360 million in military materiel ranging from radios to radar systems.

In March, the United Arab Emirates sent security forces into neighboring Bahrain to help put down pro-democracy protests. Early the next month, UAE security forces disappeared leading human rights activist Ahmed Mansoor and, in the days thereafter, detained at least four other prominent democracy activists. Before the month was out, however, the Obama administration announced its intention to arm the UAE with advanced Sidewinder tactical missiles.

Saudi Arabia also sent troops into Bahrain and has been cracking down on nonviolent activists at home with increasing vigor. The same month that, for example, Human Rights Watch reported the arrest of "at least 20 peaceful protesters, including two bloggers," the Obama administration notified Congress of its intent to see that the Saudi security forces receive $330 million worth of advanced night vision and thermal-imaging equipment.

In 2011, U.S.-coordinated arms sales resulted in the delivery of helicopter gunships to Yemen, navy patrol boats to Iraq, and the first of six cargo aircraft to the UAE. (Used armored personnel carriers were also refurbished for shipment to Iraq.)

"Reset" rhetoric aside, the president and the Pentagon are already on the record. Since 2009, they have sought to arm some of the most anti-democratic regimes on the planet, while repeatedly highlighting the need for democratic reform and now for a fresh start in the region. The Pentagon is also leaning ever more heavily on rich rulers in the Arab world to prop up the military-corporate complex at home.

In June 2009, President Obama traveled to Cairo University to give a heavily hyped and much-lauded speech ("On a New Beginning") to "the Muslim world." In his remarks, the president spoke of an American Cold-War-era attitude "in which Muslim-majority countries were too often treated as proxies without regard to their own aspirations." Then came his first call for a reset of sorts in the region. "I've come here to Cairo," he said, "to seek a new beginning between the United States and Muslims around the world, one based on mutual interest and mutual respect." Before that summer was out, however, Obama notified Congress of his intent to send Cold War-era autocrat Hosni Mubarak a shipment of new helicopters to beef up his security forces.

During that speech, Obama talked of his "unyielding belief" that all people yearn for free speech, a say in their governance, the rule of law, freedom from corruption, and other basic civil liberties. These weren't just American ideals, the president insisted, they were human rights. "And that is why we will support them everywhere," he said to waves of applause. In its actions, however, the Obama administration almost immediately left its reset rhetoric in the dust.

5.

The Pentagon's Training Missions

As the Arab Spring blossomed and President Obama hesitated about whether to speak out in favor of protesters seeking democratic change in the Greater Middle East, the Pentagon acted decisively. It forged ever deeper ties with some of the most repressive regimes in the region, building up military bases and brokering weapons sales and transfers to despots from Bahrain to Yemen.

As state security forces across the region cracked down on democratic dissent, the Pentagon also repeatedly dispatched American troops on training missions to allied militaries there. During more than 40 such operations with names like Eager Lion and Friendship Two that sometimes lasted for weeks or months at a time, they taught Middle Eastern security forces the finer points of counterinsurgency, small unit tactics, intelligence gathering, and information operations — skills crucial to defeating popular uprisings.

These recurrent joint-training exercises, seldom reported in the media and rarely mentioned outside the military, constitute the core of an elaborate, longstanding system that binds the Pentagon to the militaries of repressive regimes across the Middle East. Although the Pentagon shrouds these exercises in secrecy, refusing to answer basic questions about their scale, scope, or cost, an investigation by TomDispatch reveals the outlines of a region-wide training program whose ambitions are large and wholly at odds with Washington's professed aims of supporting democratic reforms in the Greater Middle East.

Lions, Marines, and Moroccans — Oh My!

On May 19, 2011, President Obama finally addressed the Arab Spring in earnest. He was unambiguous about standing with the protesters and against repressive governments, asserting that "America's interests are not hostile to people's hopes; they're essential to them."

Four days earlier, the very demonstrators the president sided with had marched in Temara, Morocco. They were heading for a facility suspected of housing a secret government interrogation facility to press for political reforms. It was then that the kingdom's security forces attacked.

"I was in a group of about 11 protesters, pursued by police in their cars," Oussama el-Khlifi, a 23-year-old protester from the capital, Rabat, told Human Rights Watch (HRW). "They forced me to say, 'Long live the king,' and they hit me on my shoulder. When I didn't fall, they clubbed me on the head and I lost consciousness. When I regained consciousness, I found myself at the hospital, with a broken nose and an injured shoulder."

About a five-hour drive south, another gathering was taking place under far more hospitable circumstances. In the seaside city of Agadir, a ceremony marking a transfer of military command was underway. "We're here to support... bilateral engagement with one of our most important allies in the region," said Colonel John Caldwell of the U.S. Marine Corps at a ceremony to mark the beginning of the second phase of African Lion, an annual joint-training exercise with Morocco's armed forces.

U.S. Africa Command (AFRICOM), the Pentagon's regional military headquarters that oversees operations in Africa, planned 13 such major joint training exercises in 2011 from Uganda to South Africa, Senegal to Ghana, including African Lion. Most U.S. training missions in the Greater Middle East are, however, carried out by Central Command (CENTCOM), which oversees wars and other military activities in 20 countries in the region.

"Annually, USCENTCOM executes more than 40 exercises with a wide range of partner nations in the region," a military spokesman told TomDispatch. "Due to host-nation sensitivities, USCENTCOM does not discuss the nature of many of our exercises outside our bilateral relationships."

Of the dozens of joint-training exercises it sponsored in these last years, CENTCOM would only acknowledge two by name: Leading Edge, a 30-nation exercise focused on counter-proliferation last held in the United Arab Emirates (UAE) in late 2010; and Eager Resolve, an annual exercise to simulate a coordinated response to a chemical, biological, radiological, nuclear, or high-yield explosive attack, involving the member states of the Gulf Cooperation Council.

However, military documents, open-source reports, and other data analyzed by TomDispatch offer a window into the training relationships that CENTCOM refused to acknowledge. While details of these missions remain sparse at best, the results are clear: during 2011, U.S. troops regularly partnered with and trained the security forces of numerous regimes that were actively beating back democratic protests and stifling dissent within their borders.

Getting Friendly With the Kingdom

In January 2011, for example, the government of Saudi Arabia curtailed what little freedom of expression existed in the kingdom by instituting severe new restrictions regarding online news and commentary by its citizens. That same month, Saudi authorities launched a crackdown on peaceful demonstrators. Shortly afterward, six Saudi men sought government recognition for the country's first political party whose professed aims, according to Human Rights Watch, included "greater democracy and protection for human rights." They were promptly arrested.

On February 19th, just three days after those arrests, U.S. and Saudi forces launched Friendship Two, a training exercise in Tabuk, Saudi Arabia. For the next 10 days, 4,100 American and Saudi troops practiced combat maneuvers and counterinsurgency tactics under an unrelenting desert sun. "This is a fantastic exercise and a fantastic venue, and we're sending a real good message out to the people of the region," insisted Major General Bob Livingston, a National Guard commander who took part in the mission. "The engagements that we have with the Saudi Arabian army affect their army, it affects our Army, but it also shows the people of the region our ability to cooperate with each other and our ability to be able to operate together."

Eager Lights and Lions

As the Arab Spring brought down U.S.-allied autocrats in Tunisia and Egypt, the Kingdom of Jordan, where criticizing King Abdullah or even peacefully protesting government policies is a crime, continued to stifle dissent. In 2010, for instance, state security forces stormed the house of 24-year-old computer science student Imad al-Din al-Ash and arrested him. His crime? An online article in which he called the king "effeminate."

In March 2011, Jordanian security forces typically failed to take action, and some even joined in, when pro-government protesters attacked peaceful activists seeking political reforms. Then came allegations that state forces had tortured Islamist activists.

That same month, U.S. troops joined Jordanian forces in Eager Light 2011, a joint exercise in Amman, the country's capital, that focused on counterinsurgency training. Then, from June 11th to June 30th, thousands of Jordanian security forces and U.S. troops undertook Eager Lion, focusing on special operations missions and irregular warfare as well as counterinsurgency.

That November, Human Rights Watch's Christoph Wilcke took Jordan to task for the trial of 150 protesters arrested in the spring on terrorism charges after a public brawl with pro-regime supporters. "Only members of the opposition face prosecution. The trial... is seriously flawed," wrote Wilcke. "It singles out Islamists on charges of terrorism and casts doubts on the kingdom's path towards genuine political reform, its commitment to the rule of law, and its stated desire to protect the rights of freedom of expression and assembly."

At around the same time, U.S. troops were wrapping up Operation Flexible Saif. For about four months, American troops had engaged in basic mentoring of the Jordanian military, according to Americans who took part, focusing on subjects ranging from the fundamentals of soldiering to the essentials of intelligence gathering.

Who Are Kuwait's Lucky Warriors?

In 2011, Kuwaiti security forces assaulted and arrested "Bidun" protesters, a minority population demanding citizenship rights after 50 years of stateless status in the oil-rich kingdom. "Kuwaiti authorities… should allow demonstrators to speak and assemble freely — as is their right," wrote Sarah Leah Whitson, Middle East director at Human Rights Watch. Kuwait also cracked down on online activists. In July, HRW's Priyanka Motaparthy wrote in *Foreign Policy* magazine that 26-year-old Nasser Abul was led, blindfolded and shackled, into a Kuwaiti courtroom. His crime, according to Motaparthy, "a few tweets… criticizing the ruling families of Bahrain as well as Saudi Arabia."

That same year, U.S. troops took part in Lucky Warrior, a four-day training exercise in Kuwait designed to hone U.S. war fighting skills particular to the region. The sparse material available from the military mentions no direct Kuwaiti involvement in Lucky Warrior, but documents examined by TomDispatch indicate that translators have been used in past versions of the exercise, suggesting the involvement of Kuwaiti and/or other Arab nations in the operation. Pentagon secrecy, however, makes it impossible to know the full extent of participation by the U.S. military's regional partners.

TomDispatch has identified other regional training operations that CENTCOM failed to acknowledge, including Steppe Eagle, an annual multilateral exercise carried out in repressive Kazakhstan which trained indigenous troops in everything from convoy missions to conducting cordon and search operations. Then there was the Falcon Air Meet, an exercise focusing on close air-support tactics that even included a bombing contest, carried out in October 2011 by U.S., Jordanian, and Turkish air forces at Shaheed Mwaffaq Salti Air Base in Jordan.

The U.S. military also conducted a seminar on public affairs and information operations with members of the Lebanese armed forces including, according to an American in attendance, a discussion of "the use of propaganda in regards to military information support operations." In addition, there was a biannual joint underwater demolitions exercise, Operation Eager Mace, carried out with Kuwaiti forces.

These training missions are only a fraction of the dozens carried out each year in secret, far from the prying eyes of the press or local populations. They are a key component of an outsized Pentagon support system that also shuttles aid and weaponry to a set of allied Middle Eastern kingdoms and autocracies. These joint missions ensure tight bonds between the U.S. military and the security forces of repressive governments throughout the region, offering Washington access and influence and the host nations of these exercises the latest military strategies, tactics, and tools of the trade at a moment when they are, or fear being, besieged by protesters seeking to tap into the democratic spirit sweeping the region.

Secrets and Lies

The U.S. military ignored TomDispatch's requests for information about whether any joint operations were postponed, rescheduled, or canceled as a result of Arab Spring protests. In August 2011, however, Agence France Presse reported that Bright Star, a biannual training exercise involving U.S. and Egyptian forces, had been canceled as a result of the popular revolt that overthrew President Mubarak.

The number of U.S. training exercises across the region disrupted by pro-democracy protests, or even basic information about the total number of the Pentagon's regional training missions, their locations, durations, and who takes part in them, remain largely unknown. CENTCOM regularly keeps such information secret from the American public, not to mention populations across the Greater Middle East.

The military also refused to comment on future exercises. There is nonetheless good reason to believe that their number will rise as regional autocrats look to beat back the forces of change. "With the end of Operation New Dawn in Iraq and the reduction of surge forces in Afghanistan, USCENTCOM exercises will continue to focus on... mutual security concerns and build upon already strong, enduring relationships within the region," a CENTCOM spokesman told TomDispatch by email.

Since pro-democracy protests and popular revolt are the "security concerns" of regimes from Saudi Arabia to Bahrain to Jordan, it is not hard to imagine just how the Pentagon's advanced training methods, its schooling in counterinsurgency tactics, and its aid in intelligence gathering techniques might be used in the future.

In the spring of 2011, as Operation African Lion proceeded and battered Moroccan protesters nursed their wounds, President Obama asserted that the United States "opposes the use of violence and repression against the people of the region" and supports basic human rights for citizens throughout the Greater Middle East. "And these rights," he added, "include free speech, the freedom of peaceful assembly, the freedom of religion, equality for men and women under the rule of law, and the right to choose your own leaders — whether you live in Baghdad or Damascus, Sanaa or Tehran."

The question remains, does the United States believe the same is true for those who live in Amman, Kuwait City, Rabat, or Riyadh? And if so, why is the Pentagon strengthening the hands of repressive rulers in those capitals?

6.

Prisons, Drones, and Black Ops in Afghanistan

In late December 2011, the lot was just a big blank: a few burgundy metal shipping containers sitting in an expanse of crushed eggshell-colored gravel inside a razor-wire-topped fence. The American military in Afghanistan doesn't want to talk about it, but one day soon, it will be a new hub for the American drone war in the Greater Middle East.

That empty lot will be a two-story concrete intelligence facility for that drone war, brightly lit and filled with powerful computers kept in climate-controlled comfort in a country where most of the population has no access to electricity. It will boast almost 7,000 square feet of offices, briefing and conference rooms, and a large "processing, exploitation, and dissemination" operations center — and, of course, it will be built with American tax dollars.

Nor is it an anomaly. Despite all the talk of drawdowns and withdrawals, there has been a years-long building boom in Afghanistan that shows little sign of abating. In early 2010, the U.S.-led International Security Assistance Force (ISAF) had nearly 400 bases in Afghanistan. A year later, Lieutenant Lauren Rago of ISAF public affairs told TomDispatch, the number topped 450.

The hush-hush, high-tech, super-secure facility at the massive air base in Kandahar is just one of many building projects the U.S. military has planned or underway in that country. While some U.S. bases are indeed closing up shop or being transferred to the Afghan government, and there's talk of combat operations slowing, as well as a withdrawal of American combat forces from Afghanistan by 2014, the U.S. military is still preparing for a much longer haul at mega-bases like Kandahar and Bagram airfields. The same is true even of some smaller camps, forward operating bases (FOBs), and combat outposts (COPs) scattered through the country's backlands. "Bagram is going through a significant transition during the next year to two years," Air Force Lieutenant Colonel Daniel Gerdes of the U.S. Army Corps of Engineers' Bagram Office told *Freedom Builder*, a Corps of Engineers publication. "We're transitioning... into a long-term, five-year, 10-year vision for the base."

Whether the U.S. military will still be in Afghanistan in five or 10 years remains to be seen, but steps are currently being taken to make that possible. U.S. military publications, plans and schematics, contracting documents, and other official data examined by TomDispatch catalog hundreds of construction projects worth billions of dollars slated to begin, continue, or conclude in 2012.

While many of these efforts are geared toward structures for Afghan forces or civilian institutions, a considerable number involve U.S. facilities, some of the most significant being dedicated to the ascendant forms of American warfare: drone operations and missions by elite special operations units. The available plans for most of these projects suggest durability. "The structures that are going in are concrete and mortar, rather than plywood and tent skins," says Gerdes. As of December 2011, his office was involved in 30 Afghan construction projects for U.S. or international coalition partners worth almost $427 million.

The Big Base Build-Up

In February 2012, the *New York Times* reported that President Obama would likely approve a plan to shift much of the U.S. effort in Afghanistan to special operations forces. These elite troops would then conduct kill/capture missions and train local troops well beyond 2014. Building efforts in the country bear this out.

A major project at Bagram Air Base, for instance, involves the construction of a special operations forces complex, a clandestine base within a base that will afford America's black ops troops secrecy and near-absolute autonomy from other U.S. and coalition forces. Begun in 2010, the $29 million project is slated to join roughly 90 locations around the country where troops from Combined Joint Special Operations Task Force-Afghanistan have been stationed.

Elsewhere on Bagram, tens of millions of dollars are being spent on projects that are less sexy but no less integral to the war effort, like paving dirt roads and upgrading drainage systems on the mega-base. In January, the U.S. military awarded a $7 million contract to a Turkish construction company to build a 24,000-square-foot command-and-control facility. Plans are also in the works for a new operations center to support tactical fighter jet missions, a new flight-line fire station, as well as more lighting and other improvements to support the American air war.

In January 2012, Afghan President Hamid Karzai ordered that the U.S.-run prison at Bagram be transferred to Afghan control. By the end of that month, the U.S. had issued a $36 million contract for the construction, within a year, of a new prison on the base. While details are sparse, plans for the detention center indicate a thoroughly modern, high-security facility complete with guard towers, advanced surveillance systems, administrative facilities, and the capacity to house about 2,000 prisoners.

At Kandahar Air Field, that new intelligence facility for the drone war will be joined by a similarly-sized structure devoted to administrative operations and maintenance tasks associated with robotic aerial missions. It will be able to accommodate as many as 180 personnel at a time. With an estimated combined price tag of up to $5 million, both buildings will be integral to Air Force and possibly CIA operations involving the MQ-1 Predator drone and its more advanced and more heavily-armed progeny, the MQ-9 Reaper.

The military is keeping information about these drone facilities under extraordinarily tight wraps. They refused to answer questions about whether, for instance, the construction of these new centers for robotic warfare are in any way related to the loss of Shamsi Air Base in neighboring Pakistan as a drone operations center, or if they signal efforts to increase the tempo of drone missions in the years ahead. The International Joint Command's chief of Intelligence, Surveillance, and Reconnaissance (ISR) operations, aware that such questions were to be posed, backed out of a planned interview with TomDispatch.

"Unfortunately our ISR chief here in the International Joint Command is going to be unable to address your questions," Lieutenant Ryan Welsh of ISAF Joint Command Media Outreach explained by email just days before the scheduled interview. He also made it clear that any question involving drone operations in Pakistan was off limits. "The issues that you raise are outside the scope under which the IJC operates, therefore we are unable to facilitate this interview request."

Whether the construction at Kandahar is designed to free up facilities elsewhere for CIA drone operations across the border in Pakistan or is related only to missions within Afghanistan, it strongly suggests a ramping up of unmanned operations. It is, however, just one facet of the ongoing construction at the air field, which also includes a $26 million project to build 11 new structures devoted to tactical vehicle maintenance at Kandahar. With two large buildings for upkeep and repairs, one devoted strictly to fixing tires, another to painting vehicles, as well as an industrial-sized car wash, and administrative and storage facilities, the big base's building boom shows no sign of flickering out.

Construction and Reconstruction

At Herat Air Base in the province of the same name bordering Turkmenistan and Iran, the U.S. is slated to begin a multimillion-dollar project to enhance its special forces' air operations. Plans are in the works to expand apron space — where aircraft can be parked, serviced, and loaded or unloaded — for helicopters and airplanes, as well as to build new taxiways and aircraft shelters.

That project was just one of nearly 130, cumulatively valued at about $1.5 billion, slated to be carried out in Herat, Helmand, and Kandahar provinces in 2012, according to Army Corps of Engineers documents. These also included efforts at Camp Tombstone and Camp Dwyer, both in Helmand Province as well as Kandahar's FOB Hadrian and FOB Wilson. The U.S. military also awarded a contract for more airfield apron space at a base in Kunduz, a new secure entrance and new roads for FOB Delaram II, and new utilities and roads at FOB Shank, while the Marines built a new chapel at Camp Bastion.

Early in the war, Forward Operating Base Sweeney, located a mile up in a mountain range in Zabul Province, was a well-outfitted, if remote, American base. After U.S. troops abandoned it, however, the base fell into disrepair. In January 2012, American troops returned in force and began rebuilding the outpost, constructing everything from new troop housing to a new storage facility. "We built a lot of buildings, we put up a lot of tents, we filled a lot of sandbags, and we increased our force protection significantly," Captain Joe Mickley, commanding officer of the soldiers taking up residence at the base, told a military reporter.

Decommission and Deconstruction

Hesco barriers are, in essence, big bags of dirt. Up to seven feet tall, made of canvas and heavy gauge wire mesh, they form protective walls around U.S. outposts all over Afghanistan. They'll take the worst of sniper rounds, rifle-propelled grenades, even mortar shells, but one thing can absolutely wreck them — the Marines' 9th Engineer Support Battalion.

At the beginning of December 2011, the 9th Engineers were building bases and filling up Hescos in Helmand Province. By the end of the month, they were tearing others down.

Wielding pickaxes, shovels, bolt-cutters, powerful rescue saws, and front-end loaders, they have begun "demilitarizing" bases, cutting countless Hescos — which cost $700 or more a pop — into heaps of jagged scrap metal and bulldozing berms in advance of the announced American withdrawal of its combat troops from Afghanistan. At Firebase Saenz, for example, Marines were bathed in a sea of crimson sparks as they sawed their way through the metal mesh and let the dirt spill out, leaving a country already haunted by the ghosts of British and Russian bases with yet another defunct foreign outpost. After Saenz, it was on to another patrol base slated for destruction.

Not all rural outposts are being torn down, however. Some are being handed over to the Afghan Army or police. And new facilities are now being built for the indigenous forces at an increasing rate. "If current projections remain accurate, we will award 18 contracts in February [2012]," Bonnie Perry, the head of contracting for the Army Corps of Engineers' Afghanistan Engineering District-South, told military reporter Karla Marshall. "Next quarter we expect that awards will remain high, with the largest number of contract awards occurring in May." One of the projects underway is a large base near Herat, which will include barracks, dining facilities, office space, and other amenities for Afghan commandos.

Tell Me How This Ends

No one should be surprised that the U.S. military is building up and tearing down bases at the same time, nor that much of the new construction is going on at mega-bases, while small outposts in the countryside are being abandoned. This is exactly what you would expect of an occupation force looking to scale back its "footprint" and end major combat operations while maintaining an ongoing presence in Afghanistan. Given the U.S. military's projected retreat to its giant bases and an increased reliance on kill/capture black-ops as well as unmanned air missions, it's also no surprise that its signature projects for 2012 included a new special operations forces compound, clandestine drone facilities, and a brand new military prison.

There's little doubt Bagram Air Base will exist in five or 10 years. Just who will be occupying it is, however, less clear. After all, in Iraq, the Obama administration negotiated for some way to station a significant military force — 10,000 or more troops — there beyond a withdrawal date that had been set in stone for years. While a token number of U.S. troops and a highly militarized State Department contingent remain there, the Iraqi government largely thwarted the American efforts.

It's less likely this will be the case in Afghanistan, but it remains possible. Still, it's clear that the military is building in that country as if an enduring American presence were a given. Whatever the outcome, vestiges of the current base-building boom, like the new prison at Bagram, will endure and become part of America's Afghan legacy.

Just who the jailers will be and who will be locked inside five or 10 years from now is, of course, unknown. But given the history — marked by torture and deaths — of the appalling treatment of inmates at Bagram and, more generally, of the brutality toward prisoners by all parties to the conflict over the years, in no scenario are the results likely to be pretty.

7.

Shadow Wars in Africa

They call it the New Spice Route, an homage to the medieval trade network that connected Europe, Africa, and Asia, even if today's "spice road" has nothing to do with cinnamon, cloves, or silks. Instead, it's a superpower's superhighway, on which trucks and ships shuttle fuel, food, and military equipment through a growing maritime and ground transportation infrastructure to a network of supply depots, tiny camps, and airfields meant to service a fast-growing U.S. military presence in Africa.

Few in the U.S. know about this superhighway, or about the dozens of training missions and joint military exercises being carried out in nations that most Americans couldn't locate on a map. Even fewer have any idea that military officials are invoking the names of Marco Polo and the Queen of Sheba as they build a bigger military footprint in Africa. It's all happening in the shadows of what in a previous imperial age was known as "the Dark Continent."

In East African ports, huge metal shipping containers arrive with the everyday necessities for a military on the make. They're then loaded onto trucks that set off down rutted roads toward dusty bases and distant outposts.

On the highway from Djibouti to Ethiopia, for example, one can see the bare outlines of this shadow war at the truck stops where local drivers take a break from their long-haul routes. The same is true in other African countries. The nodes of the network tell part of the story: Manda Bay, Garissa, and Mombasa in Kenya; Kampala and Entebbe in Uganda; Bangui and Djema in the Central African Republic; Nzara in South Sudan; Dire Dawa in Ethiopia; and the Pentagon's showpiece African base, Camp Lemonnier, in Djibouti on the coast of the Gulf of Aden, among others.

According to Pat Barnes, a spokesman for U.S. Africa Command (AFRICOM), Camp Lemonnier serves as the only official U.S. base on the continent. "There are more than 2,000 U.S. personnel stationed there," he told TomDispatch by email. "The primary AFRICOM organization at Camp Lemonnier is Combined Joint Task Force-Horn of Africa (CJTF-HOA). CJTF-HOA's efforts are focused in East Africa and they work with partner nations to assist them in strengthening their defense capabilities."

Barnes also noted that Department of Defense personnel are assigned to U.S. embassies across Africa, including 21 individual Offices of Security Cooperation responsible for facilitating military-to-military activities with "partner nations." He characterized the forces involved as small teams carrying out pinpoint missions. Barnes did admit that in "several locations in Africa, AFRICOM has a small and temporary presence of personnel. In all cases, these military personnel are guests within host-nation facilities, and work alongside or coordinate with host-nation personnel."

Shadow Wars

In 2003, when CJTF-HOA was first set up there, it was indeed true that the only major U.S. outpost in Africa was Camp Lemonnier. In the ensuing years, in quiet and largely unnoticed ways, the Pentagon and the CIA have been spreading their forces across the continent. Today — official designations aside — the U.S. maintains a surprising number of bases in Africa. And "strengthening" African armies turns out to be a truly elastic rubric for what's going on.

Under President Obama, in fact, operations in Africa have accelerated far beyond the more limited interventions of the Bush years: a war in Libya; a regional drone campaign with missions run out of airports and bases in Djibouti, Ethiopia, and the Indian Ocean archipelago nation of Seychelles; a flotilla of 30 ships in that ocean supporting regional operations; a multi-pronged military and CIA campaign against militants in Somalia, including intelligence operations, training for Somali agents, a secret prison, helicopter attacks, and U.S. commando raids; a massive influx of cash for counterterrorism operations across East Africa; a possible old-fashioned air war, carried out on the sly in the region using manned aircraft; tens of millions of dollars in arms for allied mercenaries and African troops; and a special ops expeditionary force (bolstered by State Department experts) dispatched to help capture or kill Lord's Resistance Army leader Joseph Kony and his senior commanders. And this only begins to scratch the surface of Washington's fast-expanding plans and activities in the region.

To support these mushrooming missions, near-constant training operations, and alliance-building joint exercises, outposts of all sorts are sprouting continent-wide, connected by a sprawling shadow logistics network. Most American bases in Africa are still small and austere, but growing ever larger and more permanent in appearance. For example, photographs of Ethiopia's Camp Gilbert, examined by TomDispatch, show a base filled with air-conditioned tents, metal shipping containers, and 55-gallon drums and other gear strapped to pallets, but also recreation facilities with TVs and videogames, and a well-appointed gym filled with stationary bikes, free weights, and other equipment.

Continental Drift

After 9/11, the U.S. military moved into three major regions in significant ways: South Asia (primarily Afghanistan), the Middle East (primarily Iraq), and the Horn of Africa. Today, the U.S. is drawing down in Afghanistan and has largely left Iraq. Africa, however, remains a growth area for the Pentagon.

The U.S. is now involved, directly and by proxy, in military and surveillance operations against an expanding list of regional enemies. They include al-Qaeda in the Islamic Maghreb in North Africa; the Islamist movement Boko Haram in Nigeria; possible al-Qaeda-linked militants in post-Qaddafi Libya; Joseph Kony's murderous Lord's Resistance Army (LRA) in the Central African Republic, Congo, and South Sudan; Mali's Islamist Rebels of the Ansar Dine; al-Shabaab in Somalia; and guerrillas from al-Qaeda in the Arabian Peninsula across the Gulf of Aden in Yemen.

A June 2012 investigation by the *Washington Post* revealed that contractor-operated surveillance aircraft based out of Entebbe, Uganda, are scouring the territory used by Kony's LRA at the Pentagon's behest, and that 100 to 200 U.S. commandos share a base with the Kenyan military at Manda Bay. Additionally, U.S. drones are being flown out of Arba Minch airport in Ethiopia and from the Seychelles Islands in the Indian Ocean, while drones and

F-15 fighter-bombers have been operating out of Camp Lemonnier as part of the shadow wars being waged by the U.S. military and the CIA in Yemen and Somalia. Surveillance planes used for spy missions over Mali, Mauritania, and the Sahara desert are also flying missions from Ouagadougou in Burkina Faso, and plans are reportedly in the works for a similar base in the newborn nation of South Sudan.

U.S. special operations forces are stationed at a string of even more shadowy forward operating posts on the continent, including one in Djema in the Central Africa Republic and others in Nzara in South Sudan and Dungu in the Democratic Republic of Congo. The U.S. also has had troops deployed in Mali, despite having officially suspended military relations with that country following a coup.

According to research by TomDispatch, the U.S. Navy also has a forward operating location, manned mostly by Seabees, Civil Affairs personnel, and force-protection troops, known as Camp Gilbert in Dire Dawa, Ethiopia. U.S. military documents indicate that there may be other even lower-profile U.S. facilities in the country. In addition to Camp Lemonnier, the U.S. military also maintains another hole-and-corner outpost in Djibouti — a Navy port facility that lacks even a name. AFRICOM did not respond to requests for further information on these posts.

Additionally, U.S. Special Operations Forces are engaged in missions against the Lord's Resistance Army from a rugged camp in Obo in the Central African Republic, but little is said about that base either. "U.S. military personnel working with regional militaries in the hunt for Joseph Kony are guests of the African security forces comprising the regional counter-LRA effort," Barnes told me. "Specifically in Obo, the troops live in a small camp and work with partner nation troops at a Ugandan facility that operates at the invitation of the government of the Central African Republic."

U.S. troops are also working at bases inside Uganda. In early 2012, elite Force Recon Marines from the Special Purpose Marine Air Ground Task Force 12 (SPMAGTF-12) trained soldiers from the Uganda People's Defense Force, which not only runs missions in the Central African Republic, but also acts as a proxy force for the U.S. in Somalia in the battle against the Islamist militants known as al-Shabaab. They now supply the majority of the troops to the African Union Mission protecting the U.S.-supported government in the Somali capital, Mogadishu.

That same spring, Marines from SPMAGTF-12 also trained soldiers from the Burundi National Defense Force (BNDF), the second-largest contingent in Somalia. In April and May, members of Task Force Raptor, 3rd Squadron, 124th Cavalry Regiment, of the Texas National Guard took part in a training mission with the BNDF in Mudubugu, Burundi.

In February 2012, SPMAGTF-12 sent trainers to Djibouti to work with an elite local army unit, while other Marines traveled to Liberia to focus on teaching riot-control techniques to Liberia's military as part of what is otherwise a State Department-directed effort to rebuild that force.

In addition, the U.S. is conducting counterterrorism training and equipping militaries in Algeria, Burkina Faso, Chad, Mauritania, Niger, and Tunisia. AFRICOM also has 14 major joint-training exercises planned for 2012, including operations in Morocco, Cameroon, Gabon, Botswana, South Africa, Lesotho, Senegal, and Nigeria.

The size of U.S. forces conducting these joint exercises and training missions fluctuates, but Barnes told me that, "on an average basis, there are approximately 5,000 U.S. Military and DoD personnel working across the continent" at any one time. In 2013, even more American troops are likely to be on hand as units from the 2nd Brigade Combat Team, 1st Infantry Division, known as the "Dagger Brigade," are scheduled to deploy to the region. The roughly 3,000 soldiers in the brigade will be involved in, among other activities, training missions while acquiring regional expertise. "Special Forces have a particular capability in this area, but not the capacity to fulfill the demand; and we think we will be able to fulfill the demand by using conventional forces," Colonel Andrew Dennis told a reporter about the deployment.

Air Africa

In June 2012, the *Washington Post* revealed that, since at least 2009, the "practice of hiring private companies to spy on huge expanses of African territory… has been a cornerstone of the U.S. military's secret activities on the continent." Dubbed Tusker Sand, the project consists of contractors flying from Entebbe airport in Uganda and a handful of other airfields. They pilot turbo-prop planes that look innocuous but are packed with sophisticated surveillance gear.

America's mercenary spies in Africa are, however, just part of the story.

While the Pentagon canceled an analogous drone surveillance program dubbed Tusker Wing, it has spent millions of dollars to upgrade the civilian airport at Arba Minch, Ethiopia, to enable drone missions to be flown from it. Infrastructure to support such operations has been relatively cheap and easy to construct, but a much more daunting problem looms — one intimately connected to the New Spice Route.

"Marco Polo wasn't just an explorer," Army planner Chris Zahner explained at a conference in Djibouti in 2011. "[H]e was also a logistician developing logistics nodes along the Silk Road. Now let's do something similar where the Queen of Sheba traveled." Paeans to bygone luminaries aside, the reasons for pouring resources into sea and ground supply networks have less to do with history than with Africa's airport infrastructure.

Of the 3,300 airfields on the continent identified in a National Geospatial-Intelligence Agency review, the Air Force has surveyed only 303 of them and just 158 of those surveys are current. Of those airfields that have been checked out, half won't support the weight of the C-130 cargo planes that the U.S. military leans heavily on to transport troops and materiel. These limitations were driven home during Natural Fire 2010, one of that year's joint training exercises hosted by AFRICOM. When C-130s were unable to use an airfield in Gulu, Uganda, an extra $3 million was spent instead to send in Chinook helicopters.

In addition, diplomatic clearances and airfield restrictions on U.S. military aircraft cost the Pentagon time and money, while often raising local suspicion and ire. In an article in the military trade publication *Army Sustainment*, Air Force Major Joseph Gaddis touts an emerging solution: outsourcing. The concept was tested during another AFRICOM training operation, Atlas Drop 2011.

"Instead of using military airlift to move equipment to and from the exercise, planners used commercial freight vendors," writes Gadddis. "This provided exercise participants with door-to-door delivery service and eliminated the need for extra personnel to channel the equipment through freight and customs areas." Using mercenary cargo carriers to skirt diplomatic clearance issues and move cargo to airports that can't accomodate C-130s is, however, just one avenue the Pentagon is pursuing to support its expanding operations in Africa.

Another is construction.

The Great Build-Up

Military contracting documents reveal plans for an investment of up to $180 million or more in construction at Camp Lemonnier alone. Chief among the projects will be the laying of 54,500 square meters of taxiways "to support medium-load aircraft" and the construction of a 185,000 square meter Combat Aircraft Loading Area. In addition, plans are in the works to erect modular maintenance structures, hangers, and ammunition storage facilities, all needed for an expanding set of secret wars in Africa.

Other contracting documents suggest that, in the years to come, the Pentagon will be investing up to $50 million in new projects at that base, Kenya's Camp Simba, and additional unspecified locations in Africa. Still other solicitation materials suggest future military construction in Egypt, where the Pentagon already maintains a medical research facility, and still more work in Djibouti.

No less telling are contracting documents indicating a future influx of "emergency troop housing" at Camp Lemonnier, including almost 300 additional Containerized Living Units (CLUs), stackable, air-conditioned living quarters, as well as latrines and laundry facilities.

Military documents also indicate that a nearly $450,000 exercise facility was installed at the U.S. base in Entebbe, Uganda, in 2011. All of this indicates that, for the Pentagon, its African build-up has only begun.

The Scramble for Africa

In a June 2012 speech in Arlington, Virginia, AFRICOM Commander General Carter Ham explained the reasoning behind U.S. operations on the continent: "The absolute imperative for the United States military [is] to protect America, Americans, and

American interests; in our case, in my case, [to] protect us from threats that may emerge from the African continent." As an example, Ham named the Somali-based al-Shabaab as a prime threat. "Why do we care about that?" he asked rhetorically. "Well, al-Qaeda is a global enterprise... we think they very clearly do present, as an al-Qaeda affiliate... a threat to America and Americans."

Fighting *them* over there, so we don't need to fight *them* here has been a core tenet of American foreign policy for decades, especially since 9/11. But trying to apply military solutions to complex political and social problems has regularly led to unforeseen consequences. For example, 2011's U.S.-supported war in Libya resulted in masses of well-armed Tuareg mercenaries, who had been fighting for Libyan autocrat Muammar Qaddafi, heading back to Mali where they helped destabilize that country. So far, the result has been a military coup by an American-trained officer; a takeover of some areas by Tuareg fighters of the National Movement for the Liberation of Azawad, who had previously raided Libyan arms depots; and other parts of the country being seized by the irregulars of Ansar Dine, the latest al-Qaeda "affiliate" on the American radar. One military intervention, in other words, led to three major instances of blowback in a neighboring country in just a year.

With the Obama administration clearly engaged in a twenty-first century scramble for Africa, the possibility of successive waves of overlapping blowback grows exponentially. Mali may only be the beginning and there's no telling how any of it will end. In the meantime, keep your eye on Africa. The U.S. military is going to make news there for years to come.

8.

Washington Puts Its Money
on Proxy War

In the 1980s, the U.S. government began funneling aid to mujahedeen rebels in Afghanistan as part of an American proxy war
against the Soviet Union. It was, in the minds of America's Cold
War leaders, a rare chance to bloody the Soviets, to give them a taste
of the sort of defeat the Vietnamese, with Soviet help, had inflicted
on Washington the decade before. In 1989, after years of bloody
combat, the Red Army did indeed limp out of Afghanistan in defeat.
Since late 2001, the United States has been fighting its former
Afghan proxies and their progeny. Now, after years of bloody combat, it's the U.S. that's looking to withdraw the bulk of its forces and
once again employ proxies to secure its interests there.

From Asia and Africa to the Middle East and the Americas, the
Obama administration is increasingly embracing a multifaceted,
light-footprint brand of warfare. Gone, for the moment at least, are

the days of full-scale invasions of the Eurasian mainland. Instead, Washington is now planning to rely ever more heavily on drones and special operations forces to fight scattered global enemies on the cheap. A centerpiece of this new American way of war is the outsourcing of fighting duties to local proxies around the world.

While the United States is currently engaged in just one outright proxy war, backing a multi-nation African force to battle Islamist militants in Somalia, it's laying the groundwork for the extensive use of surrogate forces in the future, training "native" troops to carry out missions — up to and including outright warfare. With this in mind and under the auspices of the Pentagon and the State Department, U.S. military personnel now take part in near-constant joint exercises and training missions around the world aimed at fostering alliances, building coalitions, and whipping surrogate forces into shape to support U.S. national security objectives.

While using slightly different methods in different regions, the basic strategy is a global one in which the U.S. will train, equip, and advise indigenous forces — generally from poor, underdeveloped nations — to do the fighting (and dying) it doesn't want to do. In the process, as small an American force as possible, including special forces operatives and air support, will be brought to bear to aid those surrogates. Like drones, proxy warfare appears to offer an easy solution to complex problems. But as Washington's 30-year debacle in Afghanistan indicates, the ultimate costs may prove both unimaginable and unimaginably high.

Start with Afghanistan itself. For more than a decade, the U.S. and its coalition partners have been training Afghan security forces in the hopes that they would take over the war there, defending U.S. and allied interests as the American-led international force draws down. Yet despite an expenditure of almost $50 billion on bringing it up to speed, the Afghan National Army and other security forces have drastically underperformed any and all expectations, year after year.

One track of the U.S. plan has been a little-talked-about proxy army run by the CIA. For years, the Agency has trained and employed six clandestine militias that operate near the cities of Kandahar, Kabul, and Jalalabad as well as in Khost, Kunar, and Paktika provinces. Working with U.S. Special Forces and controlled by Americans, these "Counterterror Pursuit Teams" evidently operate free of any Afghan governmental supervision and have reportedly carried out cross-border raids into Pakistan, offering their American patrons a classic benefit of proxy warfare: plausible deniability.

This clandestine effort has also been supplemented by the creation of a massive, conventional indigenous security force. While officially under Afghan government control, these military and police forces are almost entirely dependent on the financial support of the U.S. and allied governments for their continued existence.

Today, the Afghan National Security Forces officially number more than 343,000, but only 7% of its army units and 9% of its police units are rated at the highest level of effectiveness. By contrast, even after more than a decade of large-scale Western aid, 95% of its recruits are still functionally illiterate.

Not surprisingly, this massive force, trained by high-priced private contractors, Western European militaries, and the United States, and backed by U.S. and coalition forces and their advanced weapons systems, has been unable to stamp out a lightly-armed, modest-sized, less-than-popular insurgency. In recent years, one of the few tasks this proxy force has seemed skilled at is shooting American and allied forces, quite often their own trainers, in increasingly common "green-on-blue" attacks.

Adding insult to injury, this poor-performing, coalition-killing force is expensive. Bought and paid for by the United States and its coalition partners, it costs between $10 billion and $12 billion each year to sustain in a country whose gross domestic product is just $18 billion. Over the long term, such a situation is untenable.

Back to the Future

Utilizing foreign surrogates is nothing new. Since ancient times, empires and nation-states have employed foreign troops and indigenous forces to wage war or have backed them when it suited their policy aims. By the nineteenth and twentieth centuries, the tactic had become *de rigueur* for colonial powers like the French who employed Senegalese, Moroccans, and other African forces in Indochina and elsewhere, and the British who regularly used Nepalese Gurkhas to wage counterinsurgencies in places ranging from Iraq and Malaya to Borneo.

By the time the United States began backing the mujahedeen in Afghanistan, it already had significant experience with proxy warfare and its perils. After World War II, the U.S. eagerly embraced foreign surrogates, generally in poor and underdeveloped countries, in the name of the Cold War. These efforts included the attempt to overthrow Fidel Castro via a proxy Cuban force that crashed and burned at the Bay of Pigs; the building of a Hmong army in Laos which ultimately lost to Communist forces there; and the bankrolling of a French war in Vietnam that failed in 1954 and then the creation of a massive army in South Vietnam that crumbled in 1975, to name just a few unsuccessful efforts.

A more recent proxy failure occurred in Iraq. For years after the 2003 invasion, American policy-makers uttered a standard mantra: "As Iraqis stand up, we will stand down." In 2011, those Iraqis basically walked off.

Between 2003 and 2011, the United States pumped tens of billions of dollars into "reconstructing" the country with around $20 billion of it going to build the Iraqi security forces. This mega-force of hundreds of thousands of soldiers and police was created from scratch to prop up the successors to the government that the United States overthrew. It was trained by and fought with the Americans and their coalition partners, but that all came to an end in December 2011.

Despite Obama administration efforts to base thousands or tens of thousands of troops in Iraq for years to come, the Iraqi government spurned Washington's overtures and sent the U.S. military packing. The Iraqi government now supports the Assad regime in Syria, and has a warm and increasingly close relationship with long-time U.S. enemy Iran. According to Iran's semiofficial Fars News Agency, the two countries have even discussed expanding their military ties.

African Shadow Wars

Despite a history of sinking billions into proxy armies that collapsed, walked away, or morphed into enemies, Washington is currently pursuing plans for proxy warfare across the globe, perhaps nowhere more aggressively than in Africa.

Operations in Africa have accelerated far beyond the more limited interventions of the Bush years. These include a war in Libya; the expansion of a growing network of supply depots, small camps, and airfields; and a special ops expeditionary force (bolstered by State Department experts) dispatched to help capture or kill Lord's Resistance Army (LRA) leader Joseph Kony and his senior commanders. (This mission against Kony is seen by some experts as a cover for a developing proxy war between the U.S. and the Islamist government of Sudan — which is accused of helping to support the LRA — and Islamists more generally.) And this only begins to scratch the surface of Washington's fast-expanding plans and activities in the region.

In Somalia, Washington has already involved itself in a multi-pronged military and CIA campaign against Islamist al-Shabaab militants that includes intelligence operations, training for Somali agents, a secret prison, helicopter attacks, and commando raids. Now, it is also backing a classic proxy war using African surrogates. The United States has become, as the *Los Angeles Times* put it, "the driving force behind the fighting in Somalia," as it trains and equips African foot soldiers to battle Shabaab militants, so U.S. forces won't have to. In a country where more than 90 Americans were killed and wounded in a 1993 debacle now known by the shorthand "Black Hawk Down," today's fighting and dying has been outsourced to African soldiers.

In 2012, for example, elite Force Recon Marines from the Special Purpose Marine Air Ground Task Force 12 (or, as a mouthful of an acronym, SPMAGTF-12) trained soldiers from the Uganda People's Defense Force. It, in turn, supplies the majority of the troops to the African Union Mission in Somalia (AMISOM) currently protecting the U.S.-supported government in that country's capital, Mogadishu.

Marines from SPMAGTF-12 also trained soldiers from the Burundi National Defense Force (BNDF), the second-largest contingent in Somalia. Members of Task Force Raptor, 3rd Squadron, 124th Cavalry Regiment, of the Texas National Guard, took part in a separate training mission with the BNDF in Mudubugu, Burundi. SPMAGTF-12 has also sent its trainers to Djibouti, another nation involved in the Somali mission, to work with an elite army unit there.

At the same time, U.S. Army troops have taken part in training members of Sierra Leone's military in preparation for their deployment to Somalia in late 2012. In June of that year, U.S. Army

Africa commander Major General David Hogg spoke encouragingly of the future of Sierra Leone's forces in conjunction with another U.S. ally, Kenya, which invaded Somalia in the fall of 2011 (and had recently joined the African Union mission there). "You will join the Kenyan forces in southern Somalia to continue to push al Shabaab and other miscreants from Somalia so it can be free of tyranny and terrorism and all the evil that comes with it," he said. "We know that you are ready and trained. You will be equipped and you will accomplish this mission with honor and dignity."

Readying allied militaries for deployment to Somalia is, however, just a fraction of the story when it comes to training indigenous forces in Africa. In 2012, for example, Marines traveled to Liberia to focus on teaching riot-control techniques to that country's military as part of what is otherwise a State Department-directed effort to rebuild its security forces.

In fact, Colonel Tom Davis of U.S. Africa Command (AFRICOM) told TomDispatch that his command had held or planned 14 major joint training exercises for 2012 and a similar number were scheduled for 2013. Even this, however, doesn't encompass the full breadth of U.S. training and advising missions in Africa. "We... conduct some type of military training or military-to-military engagement or activity with nearly every country on the African continent," he wrote.

Our American Proxies

Africa may, at present, be the prime location for the development of proxy warfare, American-style, but it's hardly the only locale where the United States is training indigenous forces to aid U.S. foreign policy aims. The Pentagon has also ramped up operations in Central and South America as well as the Caribbean.

In Honduras, for example, small teams of U.S. troops are working with local forces to escalate the drug war there. They have taken part in joint operations with Honduran troops as part of a training mission dubbed Beyond the Horizon 2012, while Green Berets have been assisting Honduran Special Operations forces in anti-smuggling operations. Additionally, an increasingly militarized Drug Enforcement Administration sent a Foreign-deployed Advisory Support Team, originally created to disrupt the poppy trade in Afghanistan, to aid Honduras's Tactical Response Team, that country's elite counternarcotics unit.

The militarization and foreign deployment of U.S. law enforcement operatives was also evident in Tradewinds 2012, a training exercise held in Barbados that June. There, members of the U.S. military and civilian law enforcement agencies joined with counterparts from Antigua and Barbuda, Bahamas, Barbados, Belize, Canada, Dominica, the Dominican Republic, Grenada, Guyana, Haiti, Jamaica, St. Kitts and Nevis, St. Lucia, St. Vincent and the Grenadines, and Suriname, as well as Trinidad and Tobago, to improve cooperation for "complex multinational security operations."

Far less visible have been training efforts by U.S. Special Operations Forces in Guyana, Uruguay, and Paraguay. In June 2012, special ops troops also took part in Fuerzas Comando, an eight-day "competition" in which the elite forces from 21 countries, including the Bahamas, Belize, Brazil, Canada, Chile, Colombia, Costa Rica, the Dominican Republic, Ecuador, El Salvador, Guatemala, Guyana, Honduras, Jamaica, Mexico, Panama, Paraguay, Peru, Trinidad and Tobago, and Uruguay, faced-off in tests of physical fitness, marksmanship, and tactical capabilities.

The U.S. military has also conducted training exercises in Guatemala, sponsored "partnership-building" missions in the Dominican Republic, El Salvador, Peru, and Panama, and reached an agreement to carry out 19 "activities" with the Colombian army in 2012 and 2013, including joint military exercises.

The Proxy Pivot

Coverage of the Obama administration's much-publicized strategic "pivot" to Asia has focused on the creation of yet more bases and new naval deployments to the region. The military (which has dropped the word pivot for "rebalancing") is, however, also planning and carrying out numerous exercises and training missions with regional allies. In fact, the Navy and Marines alone already reportedly engage in more than 170 bilateral and multilateral exercises with Asia-Pacific nations each year.

One of the largest of these efforts took place in and around the Hawaiian Islands. Dubbed RIMPAC 2012, the exercise brought together more than 40 ships and submarines, more than 200 aircraft, and 25,000 personnel from 22 nations, including Australia, India, Indonesia, Japan, Malaysia, New Zealand, Philippines, Singapore, South Korea, Thailand, and Tonga.

Almost 7,000 American troops also joined around 3,400 Thai forces, as well as military personnel from Indonesia, Japan, Malaysia, Singapore, and South Korea as part of Cobra Gold 2012. In addition, U.S. Marines took part in Hamel 2012, a multinational training exercise involving members of the Australian and New Zealand militaries, while other American troops joined the Armed Forces of the Philippines for Exercise Balikatan.

The effects of the "pivot" are also evident in the fact that once neutralist India now holds more than 50 military exercises with the United States each year — more than any other country in the world. "Our partnership with India is a key part of our rebalance to the Asia-Pacific and, we believe, to the broader security and prosperity of the 21st century," said Deputy Secretary of Defense Ashton Carter on a 2012 trip to the subcontinent. Just how broad is evident in the fact that India is taking part in America's proxy effort in Somalia. In recent years, the Indian Navy has emerged as an "important contributor" to the international counter-piracy effort off that African country's coast, according to Andrew Shapiro of the State Department's Bureau of Political-Military Affairs.

Peace by Proxy

India's neighbor Bangladesh offers a further window into U.S. efforts to build proxy forces to serve American interests.

In 2012, U.S. and Bangladeshi forces took part in an exercise focused on logistics, planning, and tactical training, codenamed Shanti Doot-3. The mission was notable in that it was part of a State Department program, supported and executed by the Pentagon, known as the Global Peace Operations Initiative (GPOI).

First implemented under George W. Bush, GPOI provides cash-strapped nations funds, equipment, logistical assistance and training to enable their militaries to become "peacekeepers" around the world. Under Bush, from the time the program was established in 2004 through 2008, more than $374 million was spent to train and equip foreign troops. Under President Obama, Congress has funded the program to the tune of $393 million, according to figures provided to TomDispatch by the State Department.

In a 2012 speech, State's Andrew Shapiro told a Washington, D.C., audience that "GPOI is particularly focusing a great deal of its efforts to support the training and equipping of peacekeepers deploying to... Somalia" and had provided "tens of millions of dollars worth of equipment for countries deploying [there]." In a blog

post he went into more detail, lauding U.S. efforts to train Djibout-
ian troops to serve as peacekeepers in Somalia and noting that the
U.S. had also provided impoverished Djibouti with radar equipment and patrol boats for offshore activities. "Djibouti is also central to our efforts to combat piracy," he wrote, "as it is on the front
line of maritime threats including piracy in the Gulf of Aden and
surrounding waters."

Djibouti and Bangladesh are hardly unique. Under the auspices of the Global Peace Operations Initiative, the U.S. has partnered with 62 nations around the globe, according to statistics
provided by the State Department. These proxies-in-training are,
not surprisingly, some of the poorest nations in their respective regions, if not the entire planet. They include Benin, Ethiopia,
Malawi, and Togo in Africa, Nepal and Pakistan in Asia, and
Guatemala and Nicaragua in the Americas.

The Changing Face of Empire

With ongoing military operations in Asia, Africa, the Middle
East and Latin America, the Obama administration has embraced
a six-point program for light-footprint warfare relying heavily on
special operations forces, drones, spies, civilian partners, cyber-
warfare, and proxy fighters. Of all the facets of this new way of
war, the training and employment of proxies has generally been
the least noticed, even though reliance on foreign forces is considered one of its prime selling points. As the State Department's
Shapiro said: "[T]he importance of these missions to the security
of the United States is often little appreciated… To put it clearly:
When these peacekeepers deploy it means that U.S. forces are less
likely to be called on to intervene." In other words, to put it even
more clearly, more dead locals, fewer dead Americans.

The evidence for this conventional wisdom, however, is lacking. And failures to learn from history in this regard have been ruinous. The training, advising, and outfitting of a proxy force in Vietnam drew the United States deeper and deeper into that doomed conflict, leading to tens of thousands of dead Americans and millions of dead Vietnamese. Support for Afghan proxies during their decade-long battle against the Soviet Union led directly to the current disastrous decade-plus American war in Afghanistan.

Right now, the U.S. is once again training, advising, and conducting joint exercises all over the world with proxy war on its mind and the concept of "unintended consequences" nowhere in sight in Washington. Whether today's proxies end up working for or against Washington's interests or even become tomorrow's enemies remains to be seen. But with so much training going on in so many destabilized regions, and so many proxy forces being armed in so many places, the chances of blowback grow greater by the day.

9.

How the United States
Creates Global Instability

It's a story that should take your breath away: the destabilization of what, in the Bush years, used to be called "the arc of instability." It involves at least 97 countries, across the bulk of the global south, much of it coinciding with the oil heartlands of the planet. A startling number of these nations are now in turmoil, and in every single one of them — from Afghanistan and Algeria to Yemen and Zambia — Washington is militarily involved, overtly or covertly, in outright war or what passes for peace.

Garrisoning the planet is just part of it. The Pentagon and U.S. intelligence services are also running covert special forces and spy operations, launching drone attacks, building bases and secret prisons, training, arming, and funding local security forces, and engaging in a host of other militarized activities right up to full-scale war. While you consider this, keep one fact in mind: the odds are that there is no longer a single nation in the arc of instability in which the United States is in no way militarily involved.

Covenant of the Arc

"Freedom is on the march in the broader Middle East," the president said in his speech. "The hope of liberty now reaches from Kabul to Baghdad to Beirut and beyond. Slowly but surely, we're helping to transform the broader Middle East from an arc of instability into an arc of freedom."

An arc of freedom. You could be forgiven if you thought that this was an excerpt from President Barack Obama's 2011 Arab Spring speech, where he said "[I]t will be the policy of the United States to... support transitions to democracy." Those were, however, the words of his predecessor George W. Bush. The giveaway is that phrase "arc of instability," a core rhetorical concept of the former president's global vision and that of his neoconservative supporters.

The dream of the Bush years was to militarily dominate that arc, which largely coincided with the area from North Africa to the Chinese border, also known as the Greater Middle East, but sometimes was said to stretch from Latin America to Southeast Asia. While the phrase has been dropped in the Obama years, when it comes to projecting military power President Obama is in the process of trumping his predecessor.

In addition to waging more wars in "arc" nations, Obama has overseen the deployment of greater numbers of special operations forces to the region, has transferred or brokered the sale of substantial quantities of weapons there, while continuing to build and expand military bases at a torrid rate, as well as training and supplying large numbers of indigenous forces. Pentagon documents and open source information indicate that there is not a single country in that arc in which U.S. military and intelligence agencies are not now active. This raises questions about just how crucial the American role has been in the region's increasing volatility and destabilization.

Flooding the Arc

Given the centrality of the arc of instability to Bush administration thinking, it was hardly surprising that it launched wars in Afghanistan and Iraq, and carried out limited strikes in three other arc states — Yemen, Pakistan, and Somalia. Nor should anyone have been shocked that it also deployed elite military forces and special operators from the Central Intelligence Agency elsewhere within the arc.

In his book *The One Percent Doctrine*, journalist Ron Suskind reported on CIA plans, unveiled in September 2001 and known as the "Worldwide Attack Matrix," for "detailed operations against terrorists in 80 countries." At about the same time, then-Secretary of Defense Donald Rumsfeld proclaimed that the nation had embarked on "a large multi-headed effort that probably spans 60 countries." By the end of the Bush years, the Pentagon would indeed have special operations forces deployed in 60 countries around the world.

It has been the Obama administration, however, that has embraced the concept far more fully and engaged the region even more broadly. In 2010, the *Washington Post* reported that the U.S. had deployed special operations forces in 75 countries, from South America to Central Asia. In 2011, however, U.S. Special Operations Command spokesman Colonel Tim Nye told me that on any given day, America's elite troops are working in about 70 countries, and that its country total by year's end would be around 120. These forces are engaged in a host of missions, from Army

Rangers involved in conventional combat in Afghanistan to the team of Navy SEALs who assassinated Osama bin Laden in Pakistan, to trainers from the Army, Navy, Air Force, and Marines within U.S. Special Operations Command working globally from the Dominican Republic to Yemen.

That same year, the United States was involved in wars in six arc-of-instability nations: Afghanistan, Iraq, Libya, Pakistan, Somalia, and Yemen. It has military personnel deployed in other arc states, including Algeria, Bahrain, Djibouti, Egypt, Israel, Jordan, Kuwait, Lebanon, Morocco, Oman, Pakistan, Qatar, Saudi Arabia, Tunisia, and the United Arab Emirates. Of these countries, Afghanistan, Bahrain, Djibouti, Iraq, Kuwait, Oman, Qatar, Saudi Arabia, and the United Arab Emirates all host U.S. military bases, while the CIA has reportedly built a secret base somewhere in the region for use in its expanded drone wars in Yemen and Somalia. It is also using already existing facilities in Djibouti, Ethiopia, and the United Arab Emirates for the same purposes, and operating a clandestine base in Somalia where it runs indigenous agents and carries out counterterrorism training for local partners.

In addition to its own military efforts, the Obama administration has also arranged for the sale of weaponry to regimes in arc states across the Middle East, including Bahrain, Egypt, Iraq, Jordan, Kuwait, Morocco, Saudi Arabia, Tunisia, the United Arab Emirates, and Yemen. It has been indoctrinating and schooling indigenous military partners through the State Department's and Pentagon's International Military Education and Training program. In 2010, it provided training to more than 7,000 students from 130 countries. "The emphasis is on the Middle East and Africa because we know that terrorism will grow, and we know that vulnerable countries are the most targeted," Kay Judkins, the program's policy manager, told the American Forces Press Service.

According to 2011 Pentagon documents, the U.S. has personnel — some in token numbers, some in more sizeable contingents — deployed in 76 other nations sometimes counted in the arc of instability: Angola, Botswana, Burundi, Cameroon, Chad, Congo, Cote d'Ivoire, Ethiopia, Gabon, Ghana, Guinea, Kenya, Liberia, Madagascar, Mali, Mauritania, Mozambique, Niger, Nigeria, Rwanda, Senegal, Sierra Leone, South Africa, Sudan, Tanzania, Togo, Uganda, Zambia, Zimbabwe, Sri Lanka, Syria, Antigua, the Bahamas, Barbados, Belize, Bolivia, Colombia, Costa Rica, Cuba, the Dominican Republic, Ecuador, El Salvador, Guatemala, Guyana, Haiti, Honduras, Jamaica, Mexico, Nicaragua, Panama, Paraguay, Peru, Suriname, Trinidad and Tobago, Uruguay, Venezuela, Albania, Bosnia and Herzegovina, Macedonia, Romania, Serbia, Kazakhstan, Kyrgyzstan, Tajikistan, Turkmenistan, Uzbekistan, Bangladesh, Myanmar, Cambodia, Indonesia, Laos, Malaysia, the Philippines, Singapore, Thailand, and Vietnam.

While arrests of 30 members of an alleged CIA spy ring in Iran in 2011 may have been, like earlier incarcerations of supposed American "spies," pure theater for internal consumption or international bargaining, there is little doubt that the U.S. is conducting covert operations there, too. In 2010, reports surfaced that U.S. black ops teams had been authorized to run missions inside that country, and spies and local proxies are almost certainly at work there as well. The next year, the *Wall Street Journal* revealed a series of "secret operations on the Iran-Iraq border" by the U.S. military and a coming CIA campaign of covert operations aimed at halting the smuggling of Iranian arms into Iraq. (It would later be reported that the United States launched increasingly sophisticated cyber attacks against Iran, beginning in 2009.)

All of this suggests that there may, in fact, not be a single nation within the arc of instability, however defined, in which the United

States is without a base or military or intelligence personnel, or where it is not running agents, sending weapons, conducting covert operations — or at war.

The Arc of History

Just after President Obama came into office in 2009, then-Director of National Intelligence Dennis Blair briefed the Senate Select Committee on Intelligence. Drawing special attention to the arc of instability, he summed up the global situation this way: "The large region from the Middle East to South Asia is the locus for many of the challenges facing the United States in the twenty-first century." Since then, as with the Bush-identified phrase "global war on terror," the Obama administration and the U.S. military have largely avoided using "arc of instability," preferring to refer to it using vaguer formulations.

During a speech at the National Defense Industrial Association's 2011 Special Operations and Low-Intensity Conflict Symposium, for example, Navy Admiral Eric Olson, then the chief of U.S. Special Operations Command, pointed toward a composite satellite image of the world at night. Before September 11, 2001, said Olson, the lit portion of the planet — the industrialized nations of the global north — were considered the key areas. Since then, he told the audience, 51 countries, almost all of them in the arc of instability, have taken precedence. "Our strategic focus," he said, " has shifted largely to the south... certainly within the special operations community, as we deal with the emerging threats from the places where the lights aren't."

In remarks at the Paul H. Nitze School of Advanced International Studies in Washington, D.C., John O. Brennan, the assistant to the president for homeland security and counterterrorism, outlined the president's National Strategy for Counterterrorism, which highlighted carrying out missions in the "Pakistan-Afghanistan region" and "a focus on specific regions, including what we might call the periphery — places like Yemen, Somalia, Iraq, and the Maghreb [northern Africa]."

"This does not," Brennan insisted, "require a 'global' war" — and indeed, despite the Bush-era terminology, it never has. While, for instance, planning for the 9/11 attacks took place in Germany and would-be shoe-bomber Richard Reid hailed from the United Kingdom, advanced, majority-white Western nations have never been American targets. The "arc" has never arced out of the global south, whose countries are assumed to be fundamentally unstable by nature and their problems fixable through military intervention.

Building Instability

A decade's evidence has made it clear that U.S. operations in the arc of instability are destabilizing. For years, to take one example, Washington has wielded military aid, military actions, and diplomatic pressure in such a way as to undermine the government of Pakistan, promote factionalism within its military and intelligence services, and stoke anti-American sentiment to remarkable levels among the country's population. (According to one survey, just 12% of Pakistanis have a positive view of the United States.)

A semi-secret drone war in that nation's tribal borderlands, involving hundreds of missile strikes and significant, if unknown levels, of civilian casualties, has been only the most polarizing of Washington's many ham-handed efforts. When it comes to that CIA-run effort, a Pew survey of Pakistanis found that 97% of respondents viewed it negatively, a figure almost impossible to achieve in any sort of polling.

In Yemen, long-time support — in the form of aid, military training, and weapons, as well as periodic air or drone strikes — for dictator Ali Abdullah Saleh led to a special relationship between the U.S. and elite Yemeni forces led by Saleh's relatives. Those units were instrumental in cracking down on the freedom struggle there, killing protesters and arresting dissenting officers who refused orders to open fire on civilians. It's hardly surprising that, even before Yemen slid into a leaderless void (after Saleh was wounded in an assassination attempt), a survey of Yemenis found — again a jaw-dropping polling figure — 99% of respondents viewed the U.S. government's relations with the Islamic world unfavorably, while just 4% "somewhat" or "strongly approved" of Saleh's cooperation with Washington.

Instead of pulling back from operations in Yemen, however, the U.S. doubled down. The CIA, with support from Saudi Arabia's intelligence service, has run local agents as well as a lethal drone campaign aimed at Islamic militants. The U.S. military carries out its own air strikes, as well as sending in trainers to work with indigenous forces, while American black ops teams launch lethal missions, often alongside Yemeni allies.

These efforts have set the stage for further ill will, political instability, and possible blowback. In 2010, a U.S. drone strike accidentally killed Jabir al-Shabwani, the son of strongman Sheikh Ali al-Shabwani. In an act of revenge, Ali repeatedly attacked of one of Yemen's largest oil pipelines, resulting in billions of dollars in lost revenue for the Yemeni government, and demanded Saleh stop cooperating with the U.S. strikes.

In Egypt and Tunisia, long-time U.S. efforts to promote what it liked to call "regional stability" — through military alliances, aid, training, and weaponry — collapsed in the face of popular movements against the U.S.-supported dictators ruling those nations. Similarly, in Bahrain, Iraq, Jordan, Kuwait, Morocco, Oman, Saudi Arabia, and the United Arab Emirates, popular protests erupted against authoritarian regimes partnered with and armed courtesy of the U.S. military. It's hardly surprising that, when asked in a survey whether President Obama had met the expectations created by his 2009 speech in Cairo, where he called for "a new beginning between the United States and Muslims around the world," only 4% of Egyptians answered yes. (The same poll found only 6% of Jordanians thought so and just 1% of Lebanese.)

A Zogby poll of respondents in six Arab countries — Egypt, Jordan, Lebanon, Morocco, Saudi Arabia, and the United Arab Emirates — found that, taking over from a president who had propelled anti-Americanism in the Muslim world to an all-time high, Obama managed to drive such attitudes even higher. Substantial majorities of Arabs in every country now view the U.S. as not contributing "to peace and stability in the Arab World."

Increasing Instability Across the Globe

U.S. interference in the arc of instability is certainly nothing new. Leaving aside current wars, over the last century, the United States has engaged in military interventions in the global south in Cambodia, Congo, Cuba, the Dominican Republic, El Salvador, Egypt, Grenada, Guatemala, Haiti, Honduras, Iraq, Kuwait, Laos, Lebanon, Libya, Panama, the Philippines, Mexico, Nicaragua, Panama, Somalia, Thailand, and Vietnam, among other places. The CIA has waged covert campaigns in many of the same countries, as well as Afghanistan, Algeria, Chile, Ecuador, Indonesia, Iran, and Syria, to name just a few.

Like George W. Bush before him, Barack Obama evidently looks out on the "unlit world" and sees a source of global volatility and danger for the United States. His answer has been to deploy U.S. military might to blunt instability, shore up allies, and protect American lives.

Despite the salient lesson of 9/11 — interventions abroad beget blowback at home — he has waged wars in response to blowback that have, in turn, generated more of the same. A Rasmussen poll indicates that most Americans differ with the president when it comes to his idea of how the U.S. should be involved abroad. Seventy-five percent of voters, for example, agreed with this proposition: "The United States should not commit its forces to military action overseas unless the cause is vital to our national interest." In addition, clear majorities of Americans are against defending Afghanistan, Iraq, Pakistan, Saudi Arabia, and a host of other arc of instability countries, even if they are attacked by outside powers.

After decades of overt and covert U.S. interventions in arc states, including more than 10 years of constant warfare, most are still poor, underdeveloped, and seemingly even more unstable. In their annual failed state index — a ranking of the most volatile nations on the planet — *Foreign Policy* and the Fund for Peace placed Iraq and Afghanistan, the two arc nations that have seen the largest military interventions by the U.S., in their top ten. Pakistan and Yemen ranked 12th and 13th, respectively, while Somalia — the site of U.S. interventions under President Bill Clinton in the 1990s, during the Bush presidency in the 2000s, and again under Obama — had the dubious honor of being number one.

For all the discussions in the United States about (armed) "nation-building efforts" in the region, what we've clearly witnessed is a decade of nation unbuilding that ended only when the peoples of various Arab lands took their futures into their own hands and their bodies out into the streets. As polling in arc nations indicates, people of the global south see the United States as promoting or sustaining, not preventing, instability, and objective measures bear out their claims. The fact that numerous popular uprisings opposing authoritarian rulers allied with the U.S. proliferated during the Arab Spring provides the strongest evidence yet of that.

With Americans balking at defending arc-of-instability nations, with clear indications that military interventions don't promote stability, and with a budget crisis of epic proportions at home, it remains to be seen what pretexts Washington will rely on to continue a failed policy — one that seems certain to make the world more volatile and put American citizens at greater risk.

10.

What the U.S. Military Can't Do

They looked like a gang of geriatric giants. Clad in *smart casual* attire — dress shirts, sweaters, jeans — and incongruous blue hospital booties, they strode "the world," stopping to stroke their chins and ponder this or that potential crisis. Among them was General Martin Dempsey, the Chairman of the Joint Chiefs of Staff, wearing a button-down shirt and jeans, without a medal or a ribbon in sight, his arms crossed, his gaze fixed. He had one foot planted firmly in Russia, the other partly in Kazakhstan, and yet the general hadn't left the friendly confines of Virginia.

In 2012, Dempsey, the other joint chiefs, and the military's regional war-fighting commanders assembled repeatedly at the Marine Corps Base in Quantico to conduct an epic war-game-meets-academic-seminar. There, a giant map of the world, larger than a basketball court, was laid out so the Pentagon's top brass could tred the planet (provided they wore scuff-preventing shoe covers) as they thought about "potential U.S. national military vulnerabilities in future conflicts," as one participant told the *New York Times*. The sight of those generals with the world underfoot was a fitting image for Washington's military ambitions, its penchant for foreign interventions, and its contempt for (non-U.S.) borders and national sovereignty.

The idea behind Dempsey's "strategic seminars" was to plan for the future, to figure out how to properly respond to developments in far-flung corners of the globe, perhaps even on the Russian-Kazakh border. On the surface, it sounded like a sensible enough way to think through solutions to future national security threats. But when you consider how the Pentagon really operates, such war-gaming undoubtedly had an absurdist quality to it. After all, global threats turn out to come in every size imaginable, from fringe Islamic movements in Africa to Mexican drug gangs. How exactly they truly threaten U.S. "national security" is often unclear — beyond some White House advisor's or general's say-so. And whatever alternatives come up in such seminars, the sensible response invariably turns out to be sending in the Marines, or the SEALs, or the drones, or some local proxies. In truth, there is no need to spend a day shuffling around a giant map in blue booties to figure it all out.

In one way or another, the U.S. military is now involved with most of the nations on Earth. Its soldiers, commandos, trainers, base builders, drone jockeys, spies, and arms dealers, as well as associated hired guns and corporate contractors, can now be found at any given moment just about everywhere on the planet. The sun never sets on its troops conducting operations, training allies, arming surrogates, schooling its own personnel, purchasing new weapons and equipment, developing fresh doctrine, implementing novel tactics, and refining their martial arts. It has submarines trolling the briny deep and aircraft carrier task forces traversing the oceans and seas, robotic drones flying constant missions and manned aircraft patrolling the skies, while above them all spy satellites circle, peering down on friend and foe alike.

Since 2001, the U.S. military has thrown everything in its arsenal, short of nuclear weapons, including hundreds of billions of dollars in weaponry, technology, bribes, you name it, at a remarkably weak set of enemies — relatively small groups of poorly-armed fighters in impoverished nations like Iraq, Afghanistan, Somalia, and Yemen — while decisively defeating none of them. With its deep pockets and long reach, its technology and training acumen, as well as the devastatingly destructive power at its command, the U.S. military should have the planet on lockdown. It should, by all rights, dominate the world just as the neoconservative dreamers of the early Bush years assumed it would.

Yet after more than a decade of war, it has failed to eliminate a minority, rag-tag Afghan insurgency with limited popular support. It trained an indigenous Afghan force that was long known for its poor performance, before it became better known for killing its American trainers. It has spent years and untold tens of millions of tax dollars chasing down assorted firebrand clerics, various terrorist "lieutenants," and a host of no-name militants belonging to al-Qaeda, mostly in the backlands of the planet. Instead of wiping out the organization and its wannabes, however, it seems mainly to have facilitated its franchising around the world.

At the same time, it has managed to paint weak regional forces like Somalia's al-Shabaab as transnational threats, then focus its resources on eradicating them, only to fail at the task. It's thrown millions of dollars in personnel, equipment, aid, and recently even troops into the task of eradicating low-level drug runners (as well as the major drug cartels), without putting a dent in the northward flow of narcotics to America's cities and suburbs. It spends billions on intelligence only to routinely find itself in the dark. It destroyed the regime of an Iraqi dictator and occupied his country, only to be fought to a standstill by ill-armed, ill-organized insurgencies, then out-maneuvered by the allies it had helped to put in power, and unceremoniously bounced from the country. It spends untold millions of dollars to train and equip elite Navy SEALs to take on poor, untrained, lightly-armed adversaries, like gun-toting Somali pirates.

And that isn't the half of it.

The U.S. military devours money and yet delivers little in the way of victories. Its personnel may be among the most talented and well-trained on the planet, its weapons and technology the most sophisticated and advanced around. And when it comes to defense budgets, it far outspends the next nine largest nations (most of which are allies) combined, let alone its enemies like the Taliban, al-Shabaab, or al-Qaeda in the Arabian Peninsula, but in the real world of warfare this turns out to add up to remarkably little. In a government filled with agencies that are routinely derided for profligacy, inefficiency, and producing poor outcomes, its record may be unmatched in terms of waste and abject failure, though that seems to faze almost no one in Washington.

For more than a decade, the U.S. military has bounced from one failed doctrine to the next. There was Donald Rumsfeld's "military lite," followed by what could have been called military heavy (though it never got a name), and then superseded by General David Petraeus's "counterinsurgency operations" (also known by its acronym COIN). This, in turn, has been succeeded by the Obama administration's bid for future military triumph: a "light footprint" combination of special ops, drones, spies, civilian soldiers, cyber-warfare, and proxy fighters. Yet whatever the method employed, one thing has been constant: successes have been fleeting, setbacks many, frustrations the name of the game, and victory MIA.

Convinced nonetheless that finding just the right formula for applying force globally is the key to success, the U.S. military is presently banking on its new six-point plan. Tomorrow, it may turn to a different war-lite mix. Somewhere down the road, it will undoubtedly again experiment with something heavier. And if history is any guide, counterinsurgency, a concept that failed the U.S. in Vietnam and was resuscitated only to fail again in Afghanistan, will one day be back in vogue. In all of this, it should be obvious, a learning curve is lacking. Any solution to America's war-fighting problems will undoubtedly require the sort of fundamental reevaluation of warfare and military might that no one in Washington is open to at the moment. It's going to take more than a few days spent shuffling around a big map in plastic shoe covers.

American politicians never tire of extolling the virtues of the U.S. military, which is now commonly hailed as "the finest fighting force in the history of the world." This claim appears grotesquely at odds with reality. Aside from triumphs over such non-powers as the tiny Caribbean island of Grenada and the small Central American nation of Panama, the U.S. military's record since World War II has been a litany of disappointments: stalemate in Korea, outright defeat in Vietnam, failures in Laos and Cambodia, debacles in Lebanon and Somalia, two wars against Iraq — both ending without victory, more than a decade of wheel-spinning in Afghanistan, and so on.

Something akin to the law of diminishing returns may be at work. The more time, effort, and treasure the U.S. invests in its military and its military adventures, the weaker the payback. In this context, the impressive power of that military may not matter a bit, if it is tasked with doing things that military might, as it has been traditionally conceived, can perhaps no longer do. Success may not be possible, whatever the circumstances, in the twenty-first-century world, and victory not even an option. Instead of trying yet again to find exactly the right formula or even reinventing warfare, perhaps the U.S. military needs to reinvent itself and its *raison d'être* if it's ever to break out of its long cycle of failure.

But don't count on it.

Instead, expect the politicians to continue to heap on the praise, Congress to continue insuring funding at levels that stagger the imagination, presidents to continue applying blunt force (even if in slightly different ways) to complex geopolitical problems, arms dealers to continue churning out wonder weapons that prove less than wondrous, and the Pentagon continuing to fail to win.

Coming off the latest series of failures, the U.S. military has leapt headlong into yet another transitional period — call it the changing face of empire — but don't expect a change in weapons, tactics, strategy, or even doctrine to yield a change in results. As the adage goes: the more things change, the more they stay the same.

A Note on the Text

The first nine chapters of this book, written between May 17, 2011 and August 9, 2012, all appeared at TomDispatch.com. They were edited, sometimes modestly updated, and trimmed of the telltale signs of the immediate moment — the "recentlys" and "next weeks" have been removed, along with a few thematic repetitions. Otherwise they remain largely as they appeared. For the record, and in case readers should wish to check out any of the essays in their original form at TomDispatch.com, below is a list of them with the dates they were posted, their full original titles, and their URLs.

One
The New Obama Doctrine, A Six-Point Plan for Global War: Special Ops, Drones, Spy Games, Civilian Soldiers, Proxy Fighters, and Cyber Warfare
June 14, 2012, http://www.tomdispatch.com/blog/175557/tomgram%3A_nick_turse%2C_the_changing_face_of_empire

Two

A Secret War in 120 Countries: The Pentagon's New Power Elite

August 3, 2011, http://www.tomdispatch.com/blog/175426/tomgram %3A_nick_turse%2C_uncovering_the_military%27s_secret_military

Three

America's Secret Empire of Drone Bases: Its Full Extent Revealed for the First Time

October 16, 2011, http://www.tomdispatch.com/blog/175454/ tomgram%3A_nick_turse%2C_mapping_america%27s_shadowy _drone_wars

Four

Obama's Reset; Arab Spring or Same Old Thing?: How the President and the Pentagon Prop Up Both Middle Eastern Despots and American Arms Dealers

May 17, 2011, http://www.tomdispatch.com/blog/175393/tomgram %3A_nick_turse%2C_obama_and_the_mideast_arms_trade

Five

Making Repression Our Business: The Pentagon's Secret Training Missions in the Middle East

December 13, 2011, http://www.tomdispatch.com/blog/175479/ tomgram%3A_nick_turse%2C_did_the_pentagon_help_strangle _the_arab_spring

Six

450 Bases and It's Not Over Yet: The Pentagon's Afghan Basing Plans for Prisons, Drones, and Black Ops

February 12, 2012, http://www.tomdispatch.com/blog/175501/ tomgram%3A_nick_turse%2C_prisons%2C_drones%2C_and_black _ops_in_afghanistan

Seven

Obama's Scramble for Africa: Secret Wars, Secret Bases, and the Pentagon's "New Spice Route" in Africa

July 12, 2012, http://www.tomdispatch.com/blog/175567/tomgram%3A_nick_turse%2C_america%27s_shadow_wars_in_africa_

Eight

Washington Puts Its Money on Proxy War: The Election Year Outsourcing that No One's Talking About

August 9, 2012, http://www.tomdispatch.com/blog/175580/tomgram%3A_nick_turse%2C_tomorrow%27s_blowback_today

Nine

Obama's Arc of Instability: Destabilizing the World One Region at a Time

September 18, 2011, http://www.tomdispatch.com/blog/175442/tomgram%3A_nick_turse%2C_how_washington_creates_global_instability

This book has no citations. The original posts at TomDispatch.com were, however, heavily footnoted in the style of the Internet — through links that led readers to our sources and also sometimes offered directions for further exploration. Linking is the first democratic form of footnoting, making sources instantly accessible to normal readers who, unlike scholars, may not have ready access to a good library. URLs in a book, however, are both cumbersome and useless. So if you want to check the sources, you'll need to go to the originals online at TomDispatch.com.

Special Thanks

Without Lannan Foundation's support for TomDispatch, for me, and for this series of articles, this book would simply not have been possible. I'm grateful for the unstinting assistance of that foundation. It made the difference.

Acknowledgments

Nine years ago, I was a graduate student who emailed short rants, intriguing links, and every once in a while, an interesting observation to an editor. After peppering the guy with material for months, he took a chance on me and gave me one of my first writing assignments. A few years later, an editor approached me about the series of articles that the first assignment had launched. He thought they could be collected, expanded, and published. They became my first book. Last year, over dinner, an editor mentioned that I ought to continue a line of articles I had started writing. It could be a series called "the changing face of empire." All of these editors, as you might already have guessed, were the same guy. Tom Engelhardt has played an outsized role in my evolution from raw grad student to investigative reporter. It's almost impossible to catalog all the ways he's influenced and guided me. Without him, this collection of articles, this book, this imprint, probably wouldn't exist. My name may be on the cover, but he's a big part of these pages, too. To say I'm grateful is an understatement.

The efforts of a host of other people have also made this book exponentially better: Andy Breslau, Taya Kitman and everyone at the Nation Institute; Anthony Arnove, who stepped up and provided Dispatch Books a home; Andy Kroll, who expertly proofed the pieces when they were new articles; Christopher Holmes, who did the same and then proofed them again in manuscript form, as did Lucy McKeon, saving me from untold small errors; Ann Jones, who encouraged me to forge ahead with this collection; my dad, who is always on the lookout for articles I might have missed; all my fellow TomDispatch writers, who have provided me with an ongoing education and fresh insights that spark my own; and above all, my wife and my world, Tam Turse.

About Nick Turse

Nick Turse is an award-winning journalist, historian, essayist, the managing editor of TomDispatch.com and a fellow at the Nation Institute. He is the co-founder and co-editor-in-chief of Dispatch Books, the author of *The Complex: How the Military Invades Our Everyday Lives* (Metropolitan Books, 2008), the editor of *The Case for Withdrawal from Afghanistan* (Verso, 2010), and the co-author of *Terminator Planet: The First History of Drone Warfare, 2001-2050* (Dispatch Books, 2012). His *Kill Anything That Moves: The Real American War in Vietnam* will be published by Metropolitan Books in 2013.

A national security reporter and historian of the Vietnam War, Turse has written for *The Los Angeles Times, The San Francisco Chronicle, The Nation, Adbusters, GOOD, Le Monde Diplomatique, In These Times, Mother Jones* and *The Village Voice*, among other print and on-line publications.

Turse, who holds a PhD in Sociomedical Sciences from Columbia University, was the recipient of a Ridenhour Prize for Investigative Reporting at the National Press Club in April 2009 and a James Aronson Award for Social Justice Journalism from Hunter College. He has previously been awarded a Guggenheim fellowship as well as fellowships at New York University's Center for the United States and the Cold War, and Harvard University's Radcliffe Institute for Advanced Study. He has also received grants from the Fund for Investigative Journalism and the Pulitzer Center for Crisis Reporting.

He is married to Tam Turse, a photographer with whom he has collaborated on several reporting projects.

About Tom Engelhardt

Tom Engelhardt created and runs the TomDispatch.com website, a project of the Nation Institute, where he is a fellow. He is the author of two collections of his TomDispatch columns, *The United States of Fear* and *The American Way of War: How Bush's Wars Became Obama's*, as well as *The End of Victory Culture*, a highly praised history of American triumphalism in the Cold War, and *The Last Days of Publishing*, a novel. Many of his TomDispatch interviews were collected in *Mission Unaccomplished: TomDispatch Interviews with American Iconoclasts and Dissenters*. He also edited *The World According to TomDispatch: America in the New Age of Empire*, a collection of pieces from his site that functioned as an alternative history of the mad Bush years.

TomDispatch is the sideline that ate his life. Before creating it he worked as an editor at Pacific News Service in the early 1970s, and, these last four decades, as an editor in book publishing. For 15 years he was senior editor at Pantheon Books, where he edited and published award-winning works ranging from Art Spiegelman's *Maus* and John Dower's *War Without Mercy* to Eduardo Galeano's *Memory of Fire* trilogy. He is now consulting editor at Metropolitan Books, as well as the cofounder and coeditor of the American Empire Project (Metropolitan Books, 2008), where he has published best-selling works by Andrew Bacevich, Noam Chomsky, and Chalmers Johnson, among others. Many of the authors whose books he has edited and published over the years write for TomDispatch.com. For a number of years, he was also a teaching fellow at the Graduate School of Journalism at the University of California, Berkeley. He is married to Nancy J. Garrity, a therapist, has two children, Maggie and Will, and one grandchild, Charlie.

About TomDispatch

Tom Engelhardt launched TomDispatch.com in October 2001 as an email publication offering commentary and collected articles from the world press. In December 2002, it gained its name, became a project of the Nation Institute, and went online as "a regular antidote to the mainstream media." The site now features three articles a week, all original. These include Engelhardt's regular commentaries as well as the work of authors ranging from Rebecca Solnit, Bill McKibben, Andrew Bacevich, Barbara Ehrenreich, and Mike Davis to Michael Klare, Adam Hochschild, Noam Chomsky, and Karen J. Greenberg. Nick Turse, who also writes for the site, is its managing editor. Andy Kroll is its associate editor and the site's economic correspondent. Timothy MacBain produces regular TomCast audio interviews with TomDispatch authors and Erika Eichelberger handles the site's social media. Christopher Holmes is its eagle-eyed proofreader. TomDispatch is intended to introduce readers to voices and perspectives from elsewhere (even when that elsewhere is here). Its mission is to connect some of the global dots regularly left unconnected by the mainstream media and to offer a clearer sense of how this imperial globe of ours actually works.

About Dispatch Books

As an editor at Pantheon Books in the 1970s and 1980s, Tom Engelhardt used to jokingly call himself publishing's "editor of last resort." His urge to rescue books and authors rejected elsewhere brought the world Eduardo Galeano's beautiful *Memory of Fire* trilogy and Art Spiegelman's Pulitzer Prize-winning *Maus*, among other notable, incendiary, and worthy works. In that spirit, he and award-winning journalist Nick Turse founded Dispatch Books, a publishing effort offering a home to authors used to operating outside the mainstream.

With an eye for well-crafted essays, illuminating long-form investigative journalism, and compelling subjects given short shrift by the big publishing houses, Engelhardt and Turse seek to provide readers with electronic and print books of conspicuous quality offering unique perspectives found nowhere else. In a world in which publishing giants take fewer and fewer risks and style regularly trumps substance, Dispatch Books aims to be the informed reader's last refuge for uncommon voices, new perspectives, and provocative critiques.

Dispatch Books' first effort, *Terminator Planet*, explored the military's increasing use of remotely piloted drones, which have turned visions of a dystopian future into an increasingly dystopian present. Now teamed with Haymarket Press, one of the leading progressive publishers in the United States, Dispatch Books exposes and analyzes the new model of U.S. warfare with *The Changing Face of Empire*.

About Haymarket Books

Haymarket Books is a nonprofit, progressive book distributor and publisher, a project of the Center for Economic Research and Social Change. We believe that activists need to take ideas, history, and politics into the many struggles for social justice today. Learning the lessons of past victories, as well as defeats, can arm a new generation of fighters for a better world. As Karl Marx said, "The philosophers have merely interpreted the world; the point however is to change it."

We take inspiration and courage from our namesakes, the Haymarket Martyrs, who gave their lives fighting for a better world. Their 1886 struggle for the eight-hour day, which gave us May Day, the international workers' holiday, reminds workers around the world that ordinary people can organize and struggle for their own liberation. These struggles continue today across the globe—struggles against oppression, exploitation, hunger, and poverty.

It was August Spies, one of the Martyrs who was targeted for being an immigrant and an anarchist, who predicted the battles being fought to this day. "If you think that by hanging us you can stamp out the labor movement," Spies told the judge, "then hang us. Here you will tread upon a spark, but here, and there, and behind you, and in front of you, and everywhere, the flames will blaze up. It is a subterranean fire. You cannot put it out. The ground is on fire upon which you stand."

We could not succeed in our publishing efforts without the generous financial support of our readers. Many people contribute to our project through the Haymarket Sustainers program, where donors receive free books in return for their monetary support. If you would like to be a part of this program, please contact us at info@haymarketbooks.org.